Eat, Pray, Tell

The Bible Reading Fellowship
15 The Chambers, Vineyard
Abingdon OX14 3FE
brf.org.uk

The Bible Reading Fellowship (BRF) is a Registered Charity (233280)

ISBN 978 0 85746 565 8
First published 2018
10 9 8 7 6 5 4 3 2 1 0
All rights reserved

Acknowledgements
Unless otherwise stated, scripture quotations are taken from The New Revised
Standard Version of the Bible, Anglicised edition, copyright © 1989, 1995 by the Division
of Christian Education of the National Council of the Churches of Christ in the United
States of America. Used by permission. All rights reserved.

Scripture quotations taken from The Holy Bible, New International Version (Anglicised
edition) copyright © 1979, 1984, 2011 by Biblica. Used by permission of Hodder &
Stoughton Publishers, a Hachette UK company. All rights reserved. 'NIV' is a registered
trademark of Biblica. UK trademark number 1448790.

Every effort has been made to trace and contact copyright owners for material used
in this resource. We apologise for any inadvertent omissions or errors, and would ask
those concerned to contact us so that full acknowledgement can be made in the future.

A catalogue record for this book is available from the British Library

Printed and bound by CPI Group (UK) Ltd, Croydon CR0 4YY

Andrew Francis

Eat, Pray, Tell

a relational approach to 21st-century mission

This book is dedicated to

Trisha Dale, in Birmingham
Angela and Donald Hughes, in Leeds
Sarah Lane Cawte, in Burnham-on-Crouch, Essex
Janet and Matt Sutton Webb, in Cullompton, Devon
Kathryn and Philip 'Mr Cricket' Walker, in Swindon, Wiltshire

all good friends and generous hosts

Contents

Acknowledgements 9

1   Introduction: Jesus' instruction to his disciples 11

Eat

2   Welcome! 21

3   The growing understanding of Christian hospitality 31

4   Eating together in Jesus-shaped mission 41

Pray

5   Bearing one another's burdens 53

6   Pray on all occasions 61

7   Be still and know 71

Tell

8   There is good news! 83

9   Learning by experience 93

10 Growing as a Jesus-shaped community 101

Becoming Jesus-shaped people

11   Shake the dust off your feet 111

12   Principles for a missionary community 123

13   Eat, pray, tell: the shape of things to come? 133

Afterword 151

Further reading 155

Notes 157

Acknowledgements

This book owes gratitude to many folks in local churches who are exploring the eat-pray-tell agenda – normally without naming it. They have responded to my Sunday preaching or speaking at conferences about hospitality, community and ethical eating. Those who have subsequently emailed – thank you! – with fuller information and more questions should find more detailed responses in these pages. Thank you for being part of this book's witness. Several folk commented on different parts of the text, as it was being drafted – thank you, too.

I am also grateful to those to whom this book is dedicated – Angela and Donald, Janet and Matt, Kathryn and Philip, Sarah and Trisha – as well as Kathy and Jeremy Thomson and many Anabaptist/Mennonite *companeros* who have helped refine my eat-pray-tell thinking. I am grateful to The Bible Reading Fellowship, their encouraging commissioning editor Mike Parsons, my patient, precise text editor Daniele Och and all the BRF team for their help, support and care in bringing this book to you.

It was in my Birmingham grandparents' home that I first witnessed so much generous hospitality and unthreatening mealtime explanation of the reign of God. Watching that repeat itself throughout my parents' lives and homes makes me aware that such shaping of life within God's provision has been a rich blessing. But it is with Janice, my partner and her adult daughter, Caroline, that we try to offer that invitation and witness to others, who in their turn help transform our faith and discipleship.

Shalom
Andrew Francis, 2017

1

Introduction:
Jesus' instruction to his disciples

We all eat. We need to eat to survive. Those of us who are affluent enough to choose what we eat can often choose who we eat with. We do that in different ways. Some of us eat with our work colleagues every day, eating our own packed lunches in a staff room or eating at shared tables in a cafeteria. Some families gather daily for their evening meal or weekly on a Sunday for lunch. Solo pensioners often rejoice in the company shared at a weekly lunch club – and so on. Whether it is a birthday or Christmas Day, many people mark such occasions with a celebratory meal. Eating is part of the fabric of life.

I write from a white British cultural context, but of course we do not have to look far to realise that the practice of eating together is at the centre of daily life across many other cultures, both in other cultural contexts within Britain and also around the world. Think of how extended families in Caribbean, East European or south Asian communities in Britain regularly gather to cook and eat together. And I have experienced this same daily habit whenever I have journeyed abroad, whether visiting North American Mennonite communities, living in Mediterranean Europe or travelling in Asia.

'Eat, pray, tell...'

It takes a hard heart to resist the image often seen on film or TV of large Mediterranean families gathered on a sun-drenched terrace, laughing and eating around a well-stocked table. How many holiday-makers who venture beyond the confines of their package-tour hotel return with stories of shared meals and others' rich hospitality? That traditional pattern of life is part of a culture stretching the length of the Mediterranean and back through Levantine history. Any reader of the classics or the Bible can find many reminders that a life involving the sharing of food was part of those cultural histories.

At the end of his earthly ministry, just before his ascension into heaven, Matthew tells of Jesus' great commission: 'Go therefore and make disciples of all nations, baptizing them... and teaching them...' (Matthew 28:19–20). Many Christians are wrestling with how to exercise that mission today. We need to (re)discover a relevant model that works in our culture now as clearly as it did for the apostles and the early church after the first Pentecost. For without mission, the Christian community will die.

Sometimes, when speaking at a conference, I invite the audience to break into small groups and share with each other the best moments in their lives. While some people will rank a solo experience as their best – standing alone on a mountain peak at sunrise or some moment of great courage or skill (or even rank stupidity) – the vast majority of people quickly recall a time that involved eating with others. Indeed, the best conversations at such conferences come not always from the seminar room but over the meal tables or in the afternoon queue for tea and scones. Our listening and learning is enhanced as we eat together.

When travelling solo across the United States between speaking appointments, I hardly ever visit a diner without someone sharing my booth and engaging me in conversation while we eat. In several of my other books, I document my similar experiences of hospitality and meal-sharing across the world, from the Americas through the Mediterranean islands to the Far East. When developing a retreat house ministry in France, I adopted the rich patterns of local hospitality, echoed in the Bible, to enable our guests – both friends and strangers – to feel welcome.

I say all this to encourage you that your life's journey and everyday experiences can enable you to reflect on Jesus' eat-pray-tell pattern of mission, and to realise this is just as relevant today.

Learning from Jesus' earthly ministry

Jesus told his disciples, 'Whatever town or village you enter, find out who in it is worthy, and stay there until you leave' (Matthew 10:11; see also Mark 6:8–13; Luke 9:1–6). That is, eating within the community would help the disciples to establish local contacts, build friendships and create bonds of trust. The disciples were then to seek the welfare of others by praying for and healing them; in other words, meeting their obvious and self-declared needs. It was only then that teaching and telling about the 'reign of God' would begin.

Jesus could hardly have advocated this pattern without the social mores of his time involving the practice of hospitality. People would welcome newcomers, whether friend or stranger, to their homes with a meal and space to sleep. Except in the worst weather, such a daily meal would normally have been outdoors and a sheltered corner of a courtyard would have been secure enough to safely sleep in.

In the New Testament, the Gospels provide us with different representations of the life of Jesus and his first followers, who came to be called Christians. The four Gospels give us four different portraits of Jesus. Matthew, Mark and Luke share a similar viewpoint; scholars call these three Gospels the synoptics, from the Greek meaning 'with one view' (or literally 'with one eye'). The Gospel of John comes from almost a generation later, drawing on a different community that was heavily influenced by Greek philosophical thought. It is hardly surprising, therefore, that the Gospels give us helpfully contrasting patterns of meals in the early Christian communities.

Despite their different perspectives, all the Gospels have a variety of references to Jesus eating with both his disciples and with others, such as Zacchaeus the collaborating tax collector (Luke 19:1–10) or the unnamed Pharisee (Luke 14:7–14). Moreover, two of the few episodes that are recorded in all four Gospels, although with variations on the details, refer to shared meals: the feeding of the multitude (Matthew 14:13–21; Mark 6:30–44; Luke 9:10–17; John 6:5–13) and the last supper (Matthew 26:17–30; Mark 14:12–25; Luke 22:7–23; John 13:1–30). Narratives of shared meals, therefore, are a central part of the Gospels' trajectory, and the feeding of the multitude and the last supper, in particular, demonstrate how 'eating together' declares the 'reign of God'.

When it comes to the rest of the New Testament, consider how often the various writers of the letters send greetings to churches by name. Such relationships would not have occurred instantly but only over time, living and ministering together, which would have naturally involved several meals and conversation. Eating together helps us build relationships within the Christian community – however diverse and in however many congregations. Part of my rich joy in travelling to different churches to preach or to speak at conferences is to share in the hospitality of others' homes.

In the 21st century, we must heed Jesus' way of doing things, but we have to recognise that our society has different cultural norms and avoid placing ourselves and others at risk as we consider an eat-pray-tell ministry. Another purpose of this book, in its later chapters, is to offer you the example and encouragement of others who are working out their eat-pray-tell reflections in practical ways.

What this means for us now

Why does this practical strategy have application for the contemporary Western church? In recent years, there has been a significant growth of literature re-examining how the practice, lifestyle and spirituality of the early church can help us live faithfully as Christians in multicultural Britain (and other countries). In many communities and regions in what was once called Christendom, the church is becoming increasingly marginalised. Fewer and fewer people have any real understanding of the Bible, of the Christian origins of our customs and festivals, or what it means to be a Christian. Many commentators and academics regard the West today as being in an era of post-Christendom.

We briefly reviewed above how shared meals are a common denominator across many cultures and were a central feature of the life and mission of Jesus and the early church, as narrated in the Gospels and New Testament letters. We can learn from the life of Mediterranean communities and church history how our festivals and faith gather both the enquirer and the faithful through the melange of hospitality, community and prayer.

My own life has been richly flavoured by many different experiences within different expressions of Jesus' radical communities. Looking back, I realise what a debt I owe to those Franciscan and Mennonite houses of welcome, to the influence of South American liberation theologians and northern hemisphere eco-feminist theologians, as well as the communities of Taizé and Iona. I have also had heroes of mine, such as Archbishop Tutu or Thomas Merton, who along with my spiritual directors helped me understand how prayer and activism must intertwine. My eat-pray-tell education was often around others' tables – so some of these encounters appear in the following pages.

We have to find ways in which others have had vibrant and transformative Christian experiences, learn from those ways and apply what we have learned in our own context, congregation and neighbourhood. In Britain, particularly in the cities, it is not hard to find someone who has been on an Alpha course. Often, whatever else their experience of the course, they will speak of a sense of welcome at the shared meal and of being listened to. Equally, in many cities, towns and suburbs, you can quickly discover those who have encountered the hospitality of Messy Church. You do not have to go far into the life of the church to realise that, despite problems with the church building, the mockery of TV comedians or the antagonism of the media in general, Christians have things to say that are relevant, life-changing and creative. Vibrant prayer and rich spirituality are far more prevalent than dry rot in British churches!

How far do you have to go in your memories and life experience to recall actively the role of those who patiently waited until you were ready with your questions in your search for truth and answers? I have many good acquaintances who bear testimony to a particular individual, such as a vicar or a pastor, or a community, such as Iona, St Michael-le-Belfry in York, Durham's Claypath URC, Yorkshire's Scargill House, Devon's Lee Abbey, Bradwell Othona, London's St Helen's Bishopsgate or Bloomsbury Baptist Church, Catholic Worker houses (and the list goes on), who brought them to a fuller understanding of Jesus' personal call to them. Someone in the *right* place at the *right* time spoke the word of life to them. Eating, praying, telling is about building the trust for that *right* moment to occur.

Recently, I was preaching a series of post-Easter sermons preparing for Pentecost that interactively invited the listeners to share together their congregation's stumbling blocks for mission. You can probably guess their answers, some of which we will return to in more detail later. In summary, many people today recognise that inviting others to church is like the parable of the sower (Matthew 13:1–23; Mark 4:1–20; Luke 8:4–15): most of the invitations, like the seeds in that story, fall on barren ground or deaf ears; some are choked by the weeds of competing demands; and so on. Going to or being part of a church has fallen outside the experience and even the wish of the vast majority of the British population. Whatever term we use to describe it, we have moved into a post-church age for nearly all our friends, colleagues and neighbours. Yet we, as believers, must continue to wrestle with Jesus' great commission, mentioned above and which we return to later.

It is no wonder that some Christian commentators recognise that the centre of world Christianity is now rooted in the global South, particularly in Africa and Asia. The contemporary Western church needs to learn directly from Christians in those communities.

My first real spiritual director was Lesslie Newbigin, a British missionary who became a bishop in the Church of South India, then later a missionary theologian for the World Council of Churches. One of the many things he taught me was always to retain a personal dialogue with those whose Christian experience was forged in the white heat of a culture different to mine. He told me how this would become even more important in the future when thinking and learning about mission. To learn from a 'far country' is a rich gift.

Tom Stuckey, a Methodist lecturer at one of my former colleges, then later president of the Methodist Conference, tells of his deep learning from travelling in Asia: 'The "far country" affected me deeply, for I found in the friendliness, deportment and dignity of the people a simple joy and grace which we in this country seem to lack.' For Tom, that manifested itself most often in the shared meals or hospitality of small Christian communities or the quiet ways in which people gathered for daily prayer before or after their day's labour.[1]

The contrast between such examples and the Sunday oriented, privatised faith that characterises much of British Christianity is obvious. It is time for a change, and the eat-pray-tell model will help you do that without fear or embarrassment.

Eat

2

Welcome!

Some Christian friends of mine in a nearby town always answer their front door with 'Welcome!' That really surprised the man from the gas board whose unscheduled visit coincided with another meeting's participants. I have visited their home for meetings and have stayed overnight, always feeling a sense of welcome there. Their words and practice marry up. But what does welcome and being welcoming mean?

The concept of welcome comes from Old English and literally means 'well coming' or 'gladly arrived'. It often drew a 'pleased to greet you' or, as we are more likely to say, 'pleased to meet you'. We are pleased when a visiting guest or a stranger has safely arrived. We welcome them.

In my childhood in Scotland in the 1950s, one always took a small gift to one's hosts which enhanced that sense of 'well coming'. We've already seen, in the Introduction, how hospitality to travellers is a virtue across different parts of the world. Until we are subjected to or live in places of violent oppression, our natural humanity is to welcome others.

Jesus' earthly ministry was epitomised by welcome. Most notably, he welcomed those devalued by society and its ruling elites – women, children, outcasts and sinners – into his inner circle of hospitality, eating and teaching. Jesus did this as a practical demonstration of his declaration of the 'reign of God' (some may prefer the older term 'kingdom of God').

'Tell me the stories of Jesus'

As a child at Sunday school, our beginners' class always seemed to sing 'Tell me the stories of Jesus'. But as I look back, I realise how many of those narratives talked of shared meals, food and hospitality – as part of a welcome. Even my barely trained Sunday school teachers made the point that this was all part of Jesus' mission.

The parable of the prodigal son – and the angry brother and the forgiving father – speaks of the welcome afforded to the returning prodigal: 'kill the fatted calf' (Luke 15:23). The account of the Syro-Phoenician woman who challenges Jesus at the meal table (Mark 7:25–30) about her daughter's healing reminds us that Jesus welcomes her intervention. In the parable of the good Samaritan, the innkeeper is commanded to welcome the beaten-up traveller until the Samaritan returns (Luke 10:25–37). Jesus affirms Mary's action as she anoints him with oil at the meal table (Matthew 26:6–13; Mark 14:3–9; Luke 7:36–50; John 12:1–8); he welcomes the honourable service of others.

No doubt every Christian has their own favourite stories of Jesus they would add to that list. When teaching at conferences, I so often find the episode involving Zacchaeus, the collaborating tax collector (Luke 19:1–10), helpful for understanding several different aspects of welcome. First, amid the throng of people, Jesus calls Zacchaeus down from the tree he had climbed in order to watch; Jesus' welcome is inclusive of those who find themselves at the margins. Second, good English translations of verse 6 in this passage use the verb 'welcome' to describe Zacchaeus' thankful response to Jesus. Third, Zacchaeus welcomes his rehabilitation, as shown by his own repentance and desire to repay others for the hurt he has caused them. Finally, by implication, Zacchaeus welcomes Jesus and the disciples to stay at his home; local custom would inevitably include a meal.

A theology of welcome

Do not worry about that word 'theology'. It literally means God-talk or, more practically, the way we explain our understanding of God's life in the world.

A key biblical concept is that of redemption. In each of the above-mentioned stories of Jesus, the individuals involved receive different forms of inclusive redemption, as Jesus in story or action declares and demonstrates the reign of God. Despite their fears or failings, Jesus welcomed them without reserve and helped them to feel affirmed by what he asked of them next.

Welcoming others without reserve, and not judging them, is a vital Jesus-style response. Incorporating this attitude as natural behaviour within our discipleship expresses our faith and theology without using words. We have to avoid becoming over-earnest, like some of the pastors in Garrison Keillor's Lake Wobegon writings, but it is better to be inclusive and warm in our welcome than stand-offish or seemingly judgemental.

On my first Sunday in Princeton, USA, I pitched up for Sunday morning worship at a large brick building, advertising robed choirs and goodness knows what, to find the front door steward looking disdainfully at my open-necked shirt and jeans, when the temperature was pushing 30°C. The next Sunday, I headed over the railway track to a small clapboard church, where Jon, the African-American senior elder, clasped my hand in welcome and reminded me to stay for coffee and cookies after worship. Guess which church in Princeton I went to every Sunday after that?

Getting our theology and practice of welcome right is very important. Recently, I was leading worship in an English United Reformed Church, when a couple of children ran joyfully up the aisle with the adult stewards who had been gathering up the collection. As I led the people in thanking God that we 'are a rainbow people, young and old' who all want to give thanks for 'these everyday blessings', one tiny child clutched on to my leg and another looked trustingly into my open eyes. Our theology of welcome is not just about the front door but about how it is woven throughout worship and liturgy.

In the early 1960s, I was accompanying my grandfather to a printer in central Birmingham. A 'gentleman of the road' stopped us, asking for money to buy food. Grandpa looked at him sternly. 'Please, don't send me to the knees bend,' the man said. We diverted past a café, where Grandpa took him in and bought him 'tea and a slice', leaving him to enjoy the warmth at a café table on a cold day. 'God bless you,' said the man. 'And you,' replied my grandfather. Later, Grandpa explained that the 'knees bend' was a soup kitchen, run by Christians, where you had to go to an hour-long prayer meeting before getting fed. Recently, I was in London and bought a coffee to take away; I had not even sipped it when a homeless girl in a Tube station begged for money to buy one too. Thanks to Grandpa, giving her my coffee rather than some coins was the natural thing to do. Did I remember to say, 'God bless you'? Our theology and practice of welcome have to learn also how to cope with the momentary or transitory encounter.

But if our theology is only worn at Sunday worship or at the midweek Bible study, will it ever become part of the fabric of our lives?

Making our guests feel at home

One of our best learning places is when visitors come to our homes. True hospitality enables visitors and guests to feel at home – and not under pressure. Christian hospitality must exemplify that.

How we welcome people and what we invite them to share are part of the fabric of this book. Another of my good friends, dubbed Mr Cricket, always says 'be incoming' when I arrive at his door – often in response to his invitation to watch cricket on his satellite TV. When

I was a pastor in northern England, I quickly learned the importance of having the teapot and caddy visibly close to the kettle as my parishioners popped their heads around my back door with a 'time for a chat?' When the Leeds team ministry I once led had a city-centre drop-in office, my first task each day was to load up the coffee machine so that anyone and everyone could be welcomed with a mug of decent filter coffee. Later, as an area minister, I found that meeting colleagues with a problem for a pub lunch somewhere off their patch was a great way of instigating the necessary conversation. It is easy to offer can-do hospitality.

I now have an increasing circle of acquaintances who are church leaders, from a variety of denominations and traditions, who are rediscovering the importance of encouraging congregational groups to eat together. Clearly the size of the group will determine both the menu and the way of eating – at the table, a fork-supper or al fresco. We need to be aware that nowadays more than ten per cent of people are vegetarian, even more are pescatarian, and some are vegan or have food allergies. We should not make anyone feel guilty or unwelcome or 'too much trouble' because of their dietary needs and choices. Unless we know our guests really well, we should heed Joppa's lesson and enable folks to choose from enough so that they can eat whatever is set before them (Acts 10:9–16).

At one clergy supper, I was asked not to drop the pile of used plates, which I had been asked to carry into the kitchen, 'as each one cost £36'. Despite our host requesting that help, their remark did not make me feel very welcome. I far prefer to have all white china and tableware (with the exception of some gifts of French earthenware and brightly coloured central American serving dishes). We buy only inexpensive tableware and glassware, so if a guest breaks a glass or drops a plate we can easily move on without any rancour or recrimination and just replace it later.

Show homes may look nice in glossy magazines but they do not reflect how extended households live. Of course, we should vacuum, clean and dust but we need to enable people to relax and enjoy wherever we are welcoming them to. Folks are coming for a conversation, coffee or a meal not to inspect us for an *Ideal Home* photo shoot or to grade us for the Michelin guide – and not be drowned with too many cushions.

In many contexts, our invitation to shared meals may mean utilising a church's premises. Think about what that means. Ensure the entrance is well lit and easily accessible – not around the back, past the dustbins and the neighbour's barking dog. Make sure that it is more than spiders who can use the toilets, by repainting washrooms and installing soap dispensers, hot water and hand dryers (or fresh towels, as at one's home). The Americans do not call it a 'comfort break' for nothing!

Becoming a mindful host

For a couple of years, I had the privilege of living in rural France while overseeing the renovation of a derelict barn into a retreat house, with three self-catering units and a communal lounge and library around a shared courtyard garden. As its ministry began and the numbers of guests grew, I became aware again of the joy of unobtrusive hosting. Welcoming new guests was an art, making them a pot of tea or coffee after their long drive south from the ferry port, while they checked in, had their comfort breaks and tested the beds. Only then did they have a million questions – and it was the right time to speak in reply.

Whether it was us or other hosts, we each prayed privately in advance for our arriving guests just as surely as we made the beds, put wine and fruit juice in the fridges, swept the terrace or got their log stove ready. The weekly communal summer barbecue or shared winter casseroles presaged many more conversations – all wrapped in the prayer and tranquillity of the Charentaise countryside. Eat, pray, tell became our cycle of serving others.

But that time in France convinced me that what I had learned as a child at home, at youth camps, as a pastor, from house-sharing and Alpha courses, is vital to that natural eat-pray-tell cycle of Christian hospitality and mission. I returned to the UK in answer to the call of Emmanuel United Reformed Church, in Haydon Wick, who believed that God was calling them to renewed mission and life together.

As we become increasingly aware of what it really means to offer Christian hospitality, we are not only learning how to be hosts ourselves but how to be better guests. Some of our close friends help us wash up after a shared meal, enjoying the camaraderie, the conversation and more coffee. Our previous dishwasher was so temperamental that we could never ask guests to load it as it would often then malfunction, occasionally causing breakages, to their embarrassment. Offering to help clear the table may be welcomed, but then criticising or reordering the kitchen is a definite no–no.

Becoming a mindful community

All of us have learned lessons from the style of hospitality offered at the above-mentioned 'knees bend' and altered our hospitality. It has to be offered without demand or expectation of particular response. Our welcome has to be inclusive and encouraging to the newcomer. Mission relies on an open, can-do approach and attitude by the whole Christian community.

In my late teens, I volunteered with The Simon Community, and subsequently with another local charity, meeting the residential needs of ex-addicts, destitute alcoholics or former prisoners. The first lesson was to learn respect – for everyone, as well as the residents' newly acquired rooms – as we soon became a community mindful of each other's different needs and lifestyles. Friends trace my lifelong campaigning for and commitment towards better mental health services and fuller housing provisions to that mindfulness of being part of that community on the margin of society.

If we have ears to hear and eyes to see, we can quickly realise that the 21st-century church in Europe is once again a community on the edge. How many of your friends, work colleagues and adult family are still committed churchgoers? Part of what has happened is that the church has become ineffective at being a Jesus-shaped community in this era of increasing materialism and social isolation. We not only need to relearn how to be that Jesus-shaped community, we need to rediscover the ways that friends, neighbours and colleagues can become part of that community.

Christians often fail to see the mission-on-their-doorstep while prioritising the more socially needy. So, across Britain there are many strong Christian initiatives to work with those almost beyond the edge of society – the homeless and those living on the streets:

- In London, the ministry of St Martin's-in-the-Fields, partly funded by its excellent basement café, is nationally renowned.
- In Leeds, the work of St George's Crypt has a widespread outreach for supportive volunteers, funds and practical resources across that city and region.
- In Scotland, the ecumenical Julius Project, inspired by the campaigning charity Housing Justice and delivered in several locations, has the practice of befriending and welcome as a central tenet of its outreach.

My personal database details another 43 church-based initiatives with homeless people across the UK – and there are more.

Based on my experience as an itinerant speaker, perhaps a majority of British Christians perceive that such outreach to the homeless is necessary, but the patterns of welcome within their congregational life do not need to be reviewed. Why is this?

We need to recommit ourselves to becoming a 'welcome-mindful' community. The problem is that regrettably many congregations are unrealistic about the gulf which exists between the general populace and the Christian community. We have to think afresh about Christian hospitality and how we begin to welcome others who may have only a distorted view, if any, about what contemporary disciples of Jesus believe, do and say. Churches need to develop a can-do lifestyle of hospitality towards friends, neighbours, newcomers and strangers, if we are serious about Jesus' mission.

Group discussion questions

1 How good is our church/congregation's welcome and hospitality?

2 When we host meals or 'welcome events' at our church, how accessible and welcoming are our buildings?

3 What helps us to create the invitation to others to eat with us? At home? At church? and so on.

3

The growing understanding of Christian hospitality

The New Testament is woven through with the practice of hospitality. If you are familiar with this second part of the Bible, you might like to pause and jot down how many occasions you can quickly recall. You already have a head start with the references in the two preceding chapters.

One of my favourite passages of the Bible from outside the Gospels is Acts 2:43–47, describing the life of the early church, just after that first Pentecost. It tells how every day the new and growing Christian community would eat together 'with glad and generous hearts'. In a society where shared meals were part of life's ritual for the Jewish people and their Roman oppressors, what the church was doing must have been pretty special to warrant such a detailed mention. They were eating 'every day' and 'together' and 'with glad and generous hearts'. The first Christians wanted to do this; they were not merely observing the protocols of the surrounding society.

Just think what happened when the repentant co-leader of the Jerusalem church, Peter, stayed at the home of the Roman centurion in seaside Joppa (Acts 10). Peter had a vision that God was offering him a world of choice of food far bigger than his kosher Jewish ideas allowed. So, Peter could eat freely with the centurion, accepting hospitality without restriction. It is easy to imagine how such an expanded view of accepting hospitality must have caused problems, even alarm, in the Jerusalem church when Peter returned to explain himself to them all, including his co-leader, James.

In my earlier book, *Hospitality and Community after Christendom*, I offered a fuller analysis of why the majority of the later New Testament references to shared meals are in Paul's letters. But the warm greetings expressed in all the letters to the respective New Testament community leaders emphasise an ongoing relationship. Given the spread and references about those New Testament communities, it is logical that the travelling apostles and their co-workers had previously received good and extended hospitality. As the Middle Eastern proverb says, 'The hand of friendship is rooted in hospitality.'

The practice of Christian hospitality grew within the early church. The letter of Hebrews, which reputable commentators believe was written to the many dispersed Jewish Christian communities, states: 'Do not neglect to show hospitality to strangers, for by doing that some have entertained angels unawares' (Hebrews 13:2). In Revelation we read: 'Listen, I am standing at the door, knocking; if you hear my voice and open the door, I will come in and eat with you, and you with me' (Revelation 3:20). If we can open the door to the risen Christ in glory and he will come in and eat with us, it is also logical that such egalitarian hospitality was normal for Christians.

Hospitality works

I was once trained to be a church historian, examining both the documentary and other evidence to draw balanced conclusions about the life and historic practice of the church. But I am also a Christian, who is animated by the Spirit's gift and the life of the small Christian community which I am now part of. We try to have no meeting without eating. Hospitality is central to our committed life together; welcome and bring-and-share tell much of who we are as Jesus' followers.

In the monastic traditions of the first few Christian centuries, the monks were hermits who lived alone for the majority of each week.

They lived by a common rule, which included a daily pattern of prayer and sometimes a requirement to welcome and provide hospitality to the passing visitor. But on Sundays and other high days and holidays, they would each walk several miles to meet centrally at a stone cross, in a cave, or in a primitive shelter or building to worship and then eat together.

I still enjoy visiting historic monasteries, whether they lie in ruins, such as Fountains Abbey in Yorkshire, or whether they are still home to monastic communities, such as Prinknash and Downside abbeys near my home or the wonderfully ecumenical monastery at Bec in Normandy. For visitors, each monastery's three distinct buildings – guesthouse, refectory and great worship sanctuary – act as a reminder that the intertwining of prayer and the sharing of good hospitality is central to their life together. They are part of the history of the Christian church, and not just its New Testament roots, and its ongoing mission.

In Chapter 1, I shared something of the rich breadth of hospitality that I have experienced. When I studied in the USA, hardly a week went by without someone, from my professors to the church folk I worshipped with on Sunday, inviting me to their home for a barbecue or supper. It helped both to earth and underline my academic studies about how the church uses food and hospitality – and how this has enhanced its mission. During that time at Princeton and since, my bookshelves have gained many volumes about Christian hospitality. What is so important is that people from many different walks of life and different kinds of church community are affirming the importance of rediscovering the power and grace of Christian hospitality.

So what have others said?

One of the world's key writers on this subject is Christine D. Pohl, an academic based in a multiracial American seminary, with campuses in different towns. Her 1999 book *Making Room: Recovering hospitality as a Christian tradition* and my personal experience of radical Christian traditions convinced me that I should spend time working on this thesis – as well as gathering and cooking for various Christian groups. Hospitality needs to be practised. When hospitality becomes second nature to us, it works so well that both guest and host benefit.

Pohl's name keeps recurring when I enter 'Christian hospitality' into my Internet search engine: both with *Making Room* as well as some of her later books, including *Living into Community: Cultivating practices that sustain us* (2012). These two titles spell out her overarching thesis: that hospitality, exemplified by sharing food and eating together, is a practice not just to be recovered from the roots of our Christianity but will be one of the graces which sustain us as followers of Jesus' way.

Other favourite hospitality and 'eating together' books are within arm's reach as I write. Josh Hunt's *Give Friday Nights to Jesus*, advocating the use of regular shared meals to build relationships, has recently been republished as *Christian Hospitality*. Douglas Webster's *Table Grace* reaffirms the centrality of 'table fellowship' (i.e. eating together) to every ministry of hospitality. Letty M. Russell's *Just Hospitality* advocates the meal table as the place from which true strategies for God's justice spring. Arthur M. Russell's *I Was A Stranger: A theology of hospitality* is just that from a broader perspective of sources.

All those books are by North American writers; on my shelf, only Tim Chesters' somewhat evangelical *A Meal with Jesus* is written from a UK perspective. But they are all can-do approaches from different ecumenical and socio-political perspectives. Recently, many UK Christians have been joyfully challenged by *Holy Habits*, by the Methodist Church's Andrew Roberts, which encourages all the practices (and more) required by an eat-pray-tell strategy.[2]

Earlier in this book I gave some pointers to contexts where eating together, so often called 'table fellowship', has been part of the natural expression of Christianity beyond the British Isles. To some US Christian communities, such as the Amish with their barn-raising meals, black churches with their chicken suppers or Midwest white American suburban churches and Sunday picnics, there has been no perceived need to write about their practices because 'it is just what we do'; elders and pastors from these three traditions have repeatedly told me this. In all these contexts, the newcomer and stranger shared the same table of opportunity as the long-standing churchgoer.

So what am I saying?

Sharing food in extended households was a natural part of life not just within the first Christian communities. The practice of the Celtic church and medieval monasteries followed that understanding of shared meals. Radical Christian communities from the Franciscans through to 16th-century Anabaptists, 17th-century Quakers, 18th-century Moravians, 19th-century Restorationists and 20th-century Catholic Worker houses shared meals together in extended households. All this is part of the fabric of everyday yet radical British Christianity, which must challenge us afresh to re-examine what it was *and* is doing.

I have documented that history far more fully in *Hospitality and Community after Christendom*, painting with larger brush strokes what that hospitality might mean in a time of advancing secularism and diminishing churchgoing. But this book focuses upon the missional nature of what eating together can and should mean. What we do in the kitchen, at the table or around the barbecue has real impact not just for our guests but for us as hosts as well. How we behave or speak when we have folks around to eat will determine the relationship which can be built together.

The food we serve, and the way we serve it, says much about our faith, too. Few churches, if any, rely upon a cordon bleu dinner-party circuit to build their missional relationships. A well-cooked supper, lunch or barbecue that allows plenty of time for listening and conversation tells people that we enjoy God's provision of both the food and our guests. I have learned well from American Mennonite friends that, once we get to know them, enabling our guests to stir the soup, prepare the salads or help lay the table blurs the distinction between host and guest. Thus, we receive from each other.

Eating well does not demand expensive ingredients or over-feeding our guests. We can learn to serve a range of good food at a sensible budget. If you want to wrestle more with the questions of how to eat ethically, I explore this more fully in *What in God's Name Are You Eating?* Every time we serve a meal, we declare something about our theology (Godwards understanding) of food and the nature of God's provision. We need to learn how to offer good but not overwhelming Christian hospitality, and shared meals are a great starting point.

Towards a theology of food

Working out what we believe about anything is more than a circular process. It is not just about 'action' and reflection in a continuous circle. This is what academics sometimes call 'praxis'.

Praxis is much more about a controlled prayerful spiral of thought and action, whether that is about our Sunday worship or our midweek shopping. We know when a particular style or piece of worship did not work well and next time we prayerfully change that (or our response to it) towards something more appropriate. The same is true with our shopping. We might buy something one week, which the family decide is not as tasty as something else, so next week we do not buy the less tasty option again. Working out how we think about God's world, or a particular part of it, such as food, is a matter of similarly refining our choice of words and thinking.

At harvest-time, a lot of churches make a lot of noise about celebrating the food which God gives us. Then during the rest of the year, many of those churches seem to hardly give a thought or thanksgiving about our food. This is poor theology.

We have only to remember the example of how God provided manna in the wilderness for the wandering children of Israel (see Exodus 16) to recognise the daily need for food provision. I often find that I shock conference-goers when I tell them that the UK's six largest supermarkets are only 24–36 hours away from empty shelves and storerooms. We do not recognise the frailty of our food supply nor the quality of provision which we so take for granted.

All good gifts around us are…? How you answered or sang to that question may say something about your age and generation. But more importantly, it declares what you think about your food provision. We need to be continually aware that all we have is from the hand of our creator God. I am grateful that I grew up in a Christian family that said grace at each day's main meal – thanking God for our food. In my household we do the same but also hold hands around the table to remind ourselves that God completes this 'circle of blessing'. We do the same at our church's meals, several times each month. This is good theology.

What this means is, whether we are inviting folks to a meal at our home or friends and neighbours to our church's summer barbecues, harvest supper or winter meals, we consistently give thanks for *and* within God's circle of blessing. In each context, we think carefully about what we serve, often using homegrown fruit and vegetables, locally grown and produced foods and fairly traded rice, pasta, tea and coffee. We want to say that we not only honour God's provision but that we respect the earth and our sisters and brothers who work the land. Together, we are developing a good theology of food and its sharing, which declares and enriches the hospitality that we offer.

Hospitality counts

For some years I had the privilege of being an executive trustee for the UK's Mennonite Trust. Mennonites are a predominantly North American, European and Asian group of Christians. Their peacemaking, community-building tradition is part of the Anabaptist heritage, rooted in the historic Radical Reformation. At the time, the UK Mennonites worked out of their London centre, which was a house of hospitality, with its library and teaching programme. Throughout the year, the residential guests and other visitors daily joined the staff team for morning coffee, noontide prayers, gardening or afternoon tea, as well as some meals. Its Jesus-shaped ministry was naturally rooted in providing consistent and good hospitality.

As a Mennonite centre volunteer host, retreat leader and regular conference speaker, I knew how much a venue enhances the experience of its guests and visitors through the quality of its welcome and hospitality. Do groups and individuals feel they are valued and well-catered for or do they feel simply tolerated? People matter, and hospitality counts. This is just as true of our congregational life, as it is of any conference centre (whether or not it has a Christian ethos).

We never get a second chance to make a first impression. If someone feels truly welcomed but not overwhelmed, they are much more receptive to the rest of what we want to offer. I learned to properly cook in a café in a busy shopping centre. Listening to what the customer wanted, cooking it quickly and delivering it with a smile brought in both regulars and newcomers. Hospitality counts – whether you are cooking breakfasts, lunchtime soup or just a mug of tea. I believe churches are in the can-do hospitality business – but too few congregations practice it.

Group discussion questions

1 What do we see as the core values of Christian hospitality and how we share food together?

2 Which are the key moments in our personal lives and in our congregational or church lives that we invite newcomers and non-family guests to join us? Why?

3 How well do you think newcomers to our congregation or as guests in our home would rate our hospitality practices?

4

Eating together in Jesus-shaped mission

My Collins dictionary definition of hospitality is 'kindness in welcoming friends or strangers to an event or a meal'. Any good search engine or Bible concordance will add New Testament references of such hospitality and the sharing of meals.

I grew up in a radical conference of churches where the annual regional missionary tea was a vital gathering. A missionary couple, during a year-long sabbatical, would speak and share images of their life-giving work. Before the evening worship celebrating our shared mission, a lavish bring-and-share tea gave friends old and new the opportunity to speak informally of our different congregational lives in our various trans-Pennine neighbourhoods. In the summer, each congregation's annual Sunday school picnic took the majority of their neighbourhood's children out for a 'jolly' and a hearty tea.

It is not many years ago that nearly every church, both urban and rural, held a harvest supper to which they invited friends, neighbours and other community leaders. Twice I have been minister of proud former Presbyterian churches, with their St Andrew's Day dinners and their Burns' Night suppers, who invited a similar list of guests to join them. For some years, I was part of the leadership team of a congregation in the north of England which held monthly Sunday lunches, when our worship was preceded by an inward procession of crock-pots, pre-cooked casseroles and apple crumbles, heading for the kitchen. All good gifts around us.

What has been your reaction to these five examples of churches eating together? Has it been 'that's great' or 'we could do that'? Or have you recoiled from the idea of such events as 'out of date' or totally impractical, given the nature of modern life? Whether it is in a congregation's leadership team or their small group meetings, prayerful discussion is needed to discern then re-engage with eating together as part of Jesus-shaped mission.

The Alpha factor

It would be a blinkered church leadership who have not prayerfully explored, then explained the merits (or not) for their congregation getting involved in the Alpha course. The course is built around a three-fold pattern of a meal together, a talk and a discussion, with each session encouraging fuller engagement with an aspect of the Christian faith. It is overtly missional, enabling participants to talk and question freely or to walk away, but ultimately it invites commitment to the way of Jesus.

While I appreciate not everyone likes some of its theological emphases nor its assumption of adequate literacy to engage with Bible reading, Alpha is sufficiently well-known nationally and regionally, and supported with professional resources, to be worth considering here. Nearly all Alpha's commentators agree that one of the significant reasons for its popularity and success is its use of hospitality – the sharing of a meal and the sense of community which that meal engenders. This is particularly true in isolating neighbourhoods, 'bedsit land' and among uber-busy metropolitan professionals.

The fact that the Alpha method is often copied by congregations, devising their own courses (for whatever reasons) with a meal underlines the adage that 'imitation is the greatest form of flattery'. The common but key factor in Alpha and its many local imitations is the sharing of a meal. People, as individuals, enquirers, sceptics or whatever, genuinely enjoy not just the food but the opportunity to eat and talk together.

Eating together in Jesus-shaped mission only requires willing hosts, candour in motive, and opportunity. Alpha, its imitators and successors demonstrate that in 21st-century Britain this is easily possible. People can readily accept the concept that churches will host meals for themselves and others.

Meeting others' needs

The Birmingham 'knees bend' mentioned in Chapter 2 is an example of how some Christian agencies used to provide hospitality. Today, the many projects meeting the needs of homeless people around the country, which I have already referred to, show that Christians have learned to be honest in their motives and not automatically expect anything in response for their service and generosity. In several forums I have participated in as leader or teacher, I have heard the increasing concern that churches may need to re-engage with soup-kitchen ministries as the gap between the haves and have-nots widens.

During World War I, the UK government started National Kitchens in most major cities, providing the poor with an inexpensive, whole-some and nutritious daily meal. In 2017, a Liverpool charity copied that model on a few dates to demonstrate that such an initiative is again needed to meet the overwhelming demand. One of the causes of the church's growth in the early centuries was because they 'fed the poor and destitute' without 'payment nor obligation'.

The incredible growth and work of the Trussell Trust in setting up food banks in many towns, cities and regions across Britain during this past decade or so, must also be noted. What must also be recognised is the widespread ecumenical support of food banks, as well as the social divisions that are causing this need. I rarely lead an urban harvest festival without some, if not all, the goods received being passed on to the local food bank. This is also becoming a popular response for neighbourhood schools' harvest celebrations, as well as churches. Jesus' injunctions to care for our neighbour (Mark 12:31) and to feed the hungry (Matthew 25:35) in our midst are being reabsorbed into everyday thinking and practice.

In several places, I have been made aware of local churches driving initiatives to create allotments on waste land, enabling in particular the poorer members of the community to grow their own vegetables cooperatively and cheaply. On our allotment field, we have a table where folks can leave their surplus produce, pots and seed trays, and occasionally their spare tools, for others to take. These are public ways in which the church can encourage others to eat well, often in company with new-found friends.

All these are pieces of Jesus-shaped mission. The activist involvement of Christians in such things declares a coherence of faith and action to non-believers. It also gives all of us further credibility when we invite folks to come, meet and eat with us.

Bring-and-share suppers

In my childhood in 1950s Scotland, I recall well-wrapped casseroles, pies and puddings were brought to church so that the congregation could share a meal. In 1960s Manchester, our church had a good kitchen, which turned out a weekly lunch, an annual harvest supper and food for festival events, parties and regional rallies, all from ingredients brought from members' pantries and allotments, as well as the local generously discounting butcher! By the 1970s and my first gigs, girlfriends and gardens (in roughly that order of independence), I was involved in an inner-city Birmingham church where young and old, poor and rich shared in our bring-and-share meals with frequent regularity.

By the 1980s and my seminary days, I was quite convinced by the earth-friendly stewardship of bring-and-share meals as an essential part of life within the Christian community. At college, we were provided with the raw ingredients, such as one egg, one sausage, one potato, one banana and one chocolate biscuit, to concoct our own Saturday evening meal. Together with my neighbour from the next apartment, Mark Wakelin (later to become president of the Methodist Conference), we would invite as many as wanted to give us their ingredients and we would cook up a feast, which we would share communally with the donors – and often their guests. It was always a 'loaves and fishes' experience: bring-and-share with the Jesus difference. We were the first *Ready Steady Cook*s.

As a parish minister, I used to offer cookery demonstrations while telling biblical narratives. It enlivened many staid women's meetings or pensioner groups to offer something more than a devotional talk. I used to buy cheap bowls and plates from our white elephant stalls, so that I could send some of my listeners home with a ready-made meal. Teaching Cub Scouts or Girl Guides how to bake bread gave them a life-skill for the future, and something to take home to share. In Leeds and Kent, local churches used to not only invite me to come and 'cook and talk' but would also invite their friends and neighbours to watch and hear – a different way to bring and share.

In my later work among Mennonites, on either side of the Atlantic, I learned that the bring-and-share principle, or pot-luck meal, was also important to their ways of becoming church. I've lost count of the number of copies of *The Best of Mennonite Fellowship Meals* or other Mennonite cookbooks I have given to new pastors in our team to encourage them in this wonderful tradition. We need to learn from the best of other traditions (in a theological and practical bring-and-share), in order that a food-sharing ministry is central to what our churches are – and not just do. Bring-and-share affirms God's provision to us all as well as everybody's can-do opportunity to be involved, even if they bring simply a couple of loaves of bread or cartons of fruit juice.

Telling it like it is

Inadvertently, the Radio 4 broadcaster and parish priest Revd Richard Coles has made a much broader audience aware of the Christian tradition of shared meals. During his brief appearances on BBC's *Celebrity Masterchef*, he spoke openly of the need to cater for others – and to do it well. Later, while publicising his second autobiographical volume *Bringing in the Sheaves*, frequent reference was made to his building a pizza oven in his vicarage garden. This gave him an easy opportunity to explain why the church now needed to host pizza parties as an alternative way to initially gathering people than expecting attendance at Sunday worship.

While I was an area minister in Kent, I oversaw a small Medway town congregation, whose buildings surrounded a sunny courtyard. A neighbour who was dissembling their old brick barbecue not only gave it to the church, but came and rebuilt it in that courtyard. Subsequently, many events featured food grilled on that barbecue. Some of the women who had been lifelong churchgoers found their more sceptical husbands volunteering to cook at the Sunday grills and also attend the worship, slipping in and out during the hymns to fire up the coals. The church's youth group grew in numbers as they developed a pattern of winter sausage sizzles.

Since I wrote about Patchway Baptist Church's ministry (near Bristol) offering a welcome dinner to new local residents,[3] several churches have emailed to tell me that they too have begun such a ministry successfully. In Chippenham, a local community church hosts a monthly Saturday lunch for local, but particularly new, residents to help build new friendships. In Swindon, the Quaker meeting hosts an annual peacemaking reflection followed by tea and cake on the Sunday before Remembrance Day; the combination of hospitality and honest reflection was enough to attract some to further explore the Quaker faith. Two radical Christian couples, who met each other at Glastonbury Festival and discovered they both lived in the same district of Gloucester, now host a monthly discussion group with a meal, for colleagues and acquaintances. The Bristol-based Urban Life network (www.urbanlife.org) bases its Theology-To-Go and (unsurprisingly) its Meals With Meaning projects around sharing food. In Wiltshire, a retired priest and friend uses both his extended family and their shared household's annual champagne-and-carols evening to attract enquiries about the meditation programme that runs in their garden's oratory. In Stroud, a couple run a monthly book group with food, focusing on just one book each school term, but ending each evening's gathering with silence around a lit candle. In west Oxfordshire, one village chapel runs a monthly café church with cooked breakfast, inviting villagers to bring their Sunday newspapers and discuss the ethical challenges of the headlining stories. Across this same area, an Internet search revealed more than 100 congregations using Alpha, and about 60 were publicising Messy Church events (see below) as part of their outreach.

Three things bind all these Christian initiatives:

- They are independent of each other and not reliant on some strategic regional planning – except that in God's mind and heart.
- All involve hospitality, welcome and eating together, despite the rich diversity of styles and intentions. Many of them are aimed at those on the margins of, or even outside, the church.
- Incidentally, they all occur within 30 or so miles of my home, demonstrating the diversity of approach being used to build a new patchwork of Christian community in a relatively small area of Britain.

No doubt, your locality would also reveal a similar rich diversity, if you wanted to research it further. The point is that each organising group or church leadership team has recognised the value of sharing a meal as a vital pattern of outreach and of building relationships with others. Some are committed to the long soak of an annual event or a one-off welcome dinner, whereas others prefer the quick dip of a monthly or more frequent gathering.

The life-giving lesson of all these examples is that they are intentional and tell it like it is. Each one is honest in its invitation; they say this is what you are coming to and that those hosting the event are Christian, albeit with some very different emphases in their faith and prayer lives.

New wineskins

Jesus reminded his followers that one cannot just patch up old ways of doing things, in his comment about 'new wineskins' (Matthew 9:17). Increasingly, greater numbers of people know little or nothing about the church. One survey since the millennium revealed that only 16% of teenagers knew the Lord's Prayer. Many of those teenagers are now becoming parents; what and how will their children learn about Jesus?

For them, the Messy Church movement might, literally, be a Godsend. Messy Church is 'a way of being church, involving fun... that helps people encounter Jesus as Lord and Saviour'. Its 'values are about being Christ-centred, for all ages, based on creativity, hospitality and celebration'. Increasingly, food and meals, not just drinks and biscuits, are becoming part of many Messy Church gatherings.[4]

For others, the increasing use of café church can be the way forward. Not all café church congregations adopt a cabaret style of MC and singers, preferring recorded music or showing clips from YouTube or MTV (though, if you do this, be aware of the copyright issues involved) . But all include conversation around tables and sharing coffee and food – often breakfast or brunch – while thinking through the headline issues of the day.

I live within a few miles of a congregation that over the course of four Sundays each month offers a worship diet of fortnightly café church, one Messy Church and one 'traditional worship, with preacher', alongside their weekly home-group programme. I believe that this congregation's approach and the use of Messy Church or café church will become as prevalent as Alpha. I will say more about both Messy Church and café church in Chapter 13. Time to reflect?

Group discussion questions

1   What is your reaction to five examples of churches eating together listed at the start of this chapter?

2   What other can-do approaches of sharing food could your congregation or home group encourage to increase your life as a community and extend your mission? How can you make these become your 'new wineskins'?

3   How many events always incorporate food in your congregation's life? Which other events could naturally introduce eating together as an expression of your Christian hospitality

Pray

5

Bearing one another's burdens

In the Gospels, we find Jesus' ministry divides into almost four equal parts (which I explain further in Chapter 13; see page 134). One of those constituent parts is Jesus' life of prayer. He also taught his disciples and other followers how to pray.

Jesus expected his disciples to pray: 'Whenever you pray, go into your room and shut the door…' (Matthew 6:6). In noting that, we should remember that Jesus never said 'go to church'. (But then there are a lot of other things which Christians expect but which Jesus never said.) The important point here is that our personal life of prayer must precede many other things – in its daily priority, too.

The instruction to 'go into your room and shut the door' demonstrates Jesus' expectation that his followers will have a practice of offering concentrated and disciplined prayer. How often do you avert your pastor, vicar or elder's enquiry about your prayer life by affirming that you pray privately when most of it is just 'arrow' prayers ('O God, help…'), rather than a disciplined and concentrated approach? The latter does require some separation from the clamour of the world around us, so going into a room and shutting the door is wise advice.

The life of prayer is part of our shared discipleship. It is part of our approach and preparation for mission.

Exploring some biblical prayer

When we have gone into our room to pray, what then? If you have been a Christian for many years, you probably have a regular practice. Those of us from the Anglican and Anabaptist communities have our own tradition's prayer books with daily liturgies to guide our morning and evening prayers. Those of us who are part of dispersed Christian communities, such as the Iona and Northumbria communities, share in the practices and daily readings advocated by them. Others of us use one of the helpful daily guides produced by The Bible Reading Fellowship (www.brf.org.uk/bible-reading) and other publishers to use the Bible as the basis for our daily prayers. Or are you one of those still feeling bereft of resources?

In the Hebrew (Old) Testament, there are many instances of the prophets, kings and Jewish leaders praying, but it is the book of Psalms in particular that gives many insights into prayer in that tradition. Traditionally, the psalms have been ascribed as the 'songs of Jewish worship' but many have great value as prayers. Let me offer four brief examples:

- Psalm 1 begins with 'Happy are those who do not follow the advice of the wicked...' – and of those who have no use for God. We are reminded immediately that there are those who reject both God and the concept of divine power at work in the world. Those who pray with strength and trust are the living antithesis of such agnosticism. We should also note that 'happy' is an everyday translation of the more biblical term 'blessed'.
- 'Be still, and know that I am God' (Psalm 46:10) invites us to recognise the grandeur and glory of God when all in the world may not be as we expect, because God 'will be exalted among' the unbelievers as God's own people acknowledge that the divine presence is actively with us.
- 'Unless the Lord builds the house, those who build it labour in vain...' (Psalm 127:1). Christians enrich the original Hebrew thinking with our trinitarian understanding. Unless we build our

lives, spiritually and practically, as God directs us through Jesus by the power of the Spirit, we are not building up a solid spiritual foundation for how we live in the world.

- Before the final half-dozen psalms of praise, Psalm 143 is often described as a psalm of help or petition, even intercession. It begins 'Hear my prayer, O Lord, give ear to my supplications in your faithfulness'. How often, as we reflect on the trials and tribulations of God's chosen people, Israel, then and now, do we recall prayer and intercession as part of their faith's fabric?

In the New Testament, the primary prayer of Jesus is the one that he teaches to his own disciples in response to their request, 'Lord, teach us to pray'. We shall return to the significance of this in Chapter 6.

Of the narratives that occur across all four Gospels, one of the most influential is the feeding of the multitude (Matthew 14:13–21; Mark 6:30–44; Luke 9:10–17; John 6:1–13). In it Jesus uses a small peasant meal to feed the masses precisely because of his belief in prayer. Jesus *took* the bread, *blessed* (prayed over) it, *broke* it and *gave* it to be shared. Have you noticed that later in his ministry, Jesus used this same fourfold pattern when he shared the last supper with his disciples? Prayer is central to sharing the blessing of the reign of God.

During Jesus' ministry, three of his closest associates were Lazarus and his two sisters, Martha and Mary. After Lazarus' death, Jesus wept on hearing the news as he got to their village. Yet Jesus himself knew that he needed to intercede in prayer with his Father in heaven before Lazarus could be raised from death (John 11:40-44).

In darkest Gethsemane, in the hours before Jesus' arrest, he enjoined his disciples to keep watch and to pray (Matthew 26:38; Luke 22:46). Jesus prayed so hard about the will of his Father in heaven that his sweat was like blood, as he wrestled with God's plan. We too need to learn to 'keep watch' in our private prayer times that we too can wrestle with God's plan, however uncomfortable its outcome for us and others.

In Acts 2:42–47, we discover the first description of the post-resurrection, post-Pentecost church. It describes the common life of the earliest New Testament church. In translations from the original manuscripts, this includes eating together and sharing in 'the breaking of bread and the prayers' (vv. 46–47).

Later in this chapter we will consider the Galatian injunction to 'bear each other's burdens', and in the next chapter the Ephesian injunction to 'pray on every occasion'. Prayer is woven through the fabric of those who accept the reign of God, ultimately made known in Jesus, then and now.

Devotio moderna

That sense of a shared common life repeats itself down through church history, particularly among those strands which see themselves as communities rather than congregations. One such influential group was the Brethren of the Common Life, the 14th-century lay Dutch pietist community which gathered round Geert Groote following his transformative religious conversion (akin to Paul's or the later John Wesley). Apart from labouring and farming to provide shelter and food, this group spent their waking hours in prayer, listening to sermons and sharing meals; this was their common life.

They became the best-known example of a new lay form of communal pietism, symbolised by their individual sharing of prayer, called *devotio moderna*. Many Reformation scholars recognise the development of this spirituality as a necessary seedbed for the various forms of reformation throughout Europe which occurred in the following centuries.

One adherent and exemplary early writer of the Brethren of the Common Life was Thomas à Kempis. His work *The Imitation of Christ* became the key text of *devotio moderna*, recognising that the work of every believer was to imitate Jesus in his words and ways, particularly in the work of prayer.

The Imitation of Christ has 116 meditations spread across four sections, built around the liturgical year. It is a manual for prayer, Christian reflection and gradual but frequent, if not daily, usage. In many ways, it seeks to engage the heart – rather than the mind – in helping everyone to build 'the pathway to empathy' in their prayers for others. Although I keep a couple of personally annotated inexpensive paperback editions of *The Imitation* for teaching and reference, one of my treasured books, kept next to my everyday Bible, is a hardback edition with modernist woodcut-style illustrations.

Recognising that, it becomes easier to understand how the more catholic church historians often find the roots of the later Carmelite movement deep in the soil of *The Imitation of Christ*. The authentic life of prayer shares traits that can be traced back through various forms of Christian 'common life', whatever its churchmanship, into those of the Bible and the first New Testament 'churches'. Sharing a 'common life' is part of our discipleship. How much do we recognise that in our own choice of resources?

'The pathway to empathy'

Allan Armstrong ODP offered me the phrase 'the pathway to empathy', referring to the 'heartset' (as against mindset) that Christians as intercessors must acquire. We need to give real understanding to others, however stumbling in their request, as they ask us to pray for their concerns.

The central thesis of this book is eat, pray, tell. The second part of this understanding involves praying for others and their concerns. Liturgically, prayers offered on behalf of others are called intercession, because one is interceding on their behalf.

When Jesus sent his disciples out to new communities, he instructed them to become part of those communities, then to meet the people there in their needs before telling them about the reign of God. One of the key ways that Jesus' followers use to meet others' needs is to pray for them. This is because as we regularly present their specific need before God, we attune our hearts and minds to the Spirit's prompting towards an appropriate level of practical support. Have you noted how this practice of meeting need is rooted primarily in prayer?

It is therefore important to ensure a pathway to empathy is part of our life's fabric if it is going to speak to others. Others will need to know us as people of prayer if they are going to trust us to pray for their deepest concerns. They have to believe not only that we empathise with them and their concern but also that we have sufficient faith in our God who hears our prayers.

Some Galatian thinking

Paul developed a mature way of thinking about communal empathy, which he explained in his letter to the Galatians. Galatians 6:2 is variously translated as 'bearing each other's burdens' and 'sharing each other's joy'. This is not just empathy but candid relationship development and practical community-building, and it is at the heart of our mission.

The several commentaries on Galatians on my bookshelf share a creative unanimity. They all agree that Paul's purpose in writing to the Galatians was to answer unknown yet obvious questions about Gentile and pagan involvement in the nascent Christian community. Should they be circumcised? If not, were they still fully Christian? And so on. What is essential is that individuals are free under God's grace to share in the blessings of that reign. The central message (Galatians 2:15–21) is that we are saved by faith in the one who can redeem even the blackest situation or individual, that is, Jesus

Christ. The Spirit, not the limitations of human nature and thinking, must determine our lives (5:16–26).

Part of the authenticity of the Galatian letter is affirmed by Paul's own style, writing and final greeting (6:11–18). But sandwiched between the advocacy about the life-determining Spirit and that final greeting is the teaching that the Christian life is about 'bearing each other's burdens'. The coherence of the Christian community is the inheritance of Jesus Christ's grace, life in the Spirit's determination and a willingness to bear each other's burdens.

This has direct relevance for our eat-pray-tell thinking. Galatians tells us that God's blessings are not limited to those from a background of faith but all are included. In exercising Jesus' pattern for mission, we can be confident that prayers made in Jesus' name are heard. But it will be the grace of Jesus and our lives shaped by his Spirit which will determine our heart for others' needs.

Praying for others' healing

Prayers made in the name of Jesus are always heard by the creator God. But this does not mean that they are always answered as we expect. God's answers to our prayers are not necessarily those of our limited human thinking and expression. Book after book, not just this one, will tell you that.

Healing is about an individual's wholeness in the sight of God. This is not limited to physical ailments, emotional needs or mental disorder. A family in not-fit-for-purpose housing has a practical need; someone working for an abusive employer may have financial shortages. This means that our prayer for others' healing may be for a different pattern of God's justice to prevail, so that their needs are met in particularly institutional ways. What it cannot mean is limiting our prayers to some kind of shopping list for God to fulfil.

Often the person doing the praying can be prompted by God's Spirit to act in particular ways, enabling earthly answers to those prayers. We only need to think of John the Baptist's 'reign of God' teaching about two coats to realise this (Luke 3:11). Praying for others to bring both God's judgement and its practical obligations upon us is an essential part of the life of discipleship. Praying for others is not simply an 'over to you, Lord' petition.

After I had led a conference session on this book's subject, one pastor stood up and repented that some of his previous teaching had not given enough recognition to our obligations when praying for others. That was humbling for everyone listening. I will never forget his last sentence before he sat down: 'Praying for others is where the rubber hits the road for our discipleship; it is the litmus test of how much we want to follow Jesus' teaching.'

Group discussion questions

1 Which is your favourite personal passage about prayer in the Bible?

2 Why is it important for our intercessions to continually develop 'a pathway to empathy'?

3 How (in this group) do we 'bear each other's burdens'?

6

Pray on all occasions

Unlike Galatians, the letter to the Ephesians helps us to recognise the untidiness of the Bible – that not every loose end can be tied. But we can first recognise the strength of the letter's affirmation that those sent by God into a mission situation have a clear obligation to pray for others (2:11—3:21). This is applied particularly to Paul, the apostle, church planter and missionary evangelist, to help set a benchmark for others with subsequent or similar ministries.

I am encouraged by the fact that the Bible does have loose ends, that it is untidy at various points and that not every 'i' is dotted and 't' crossed. It adds to both its wonder and its strength as witness. Would you want every witness statement to an actual event to be identical? I am grateful that in my successive degree studies in theology, I have continued to learn how to question and cross-examine biblical scholarship to reveal the character of the Bible's teaching.

There is a growing school of thought that the letter to the Ephesians is neo-Pauline. That is, it reflects his pattern of thinking but was not written by him (unlike, say, Galatians or Romans), but by one or more of his trusted co-workers. Scholars recognise this by the different use of some words or linguistic phrases as well as its impersonal justification for Paul's style of ministry. None of this belittles its scriptural value or its place in the Bible or canon but enriches the application of Pauline thinking to our 21st-century mission, because of the 'common life' approach of those Pauline congregations.

For those of us from an Anabaptist, or specifically Mennonite, Christian background, Ephesians has particular significance. Whoever wrote it was exhorting the Ephesian Christians not to break into further factions but to be prepared to live in submission to one another as we all should live in submission to Jesus' words and ways. The historic Anabaptist value of 'yieldedness' (a translation of the German *Gelassenheit*), which typifies this movement, to each other, to our local church and to the God we know in Jesus, is underpinned by Ephesians, as well as by the Galatian 'bear each other's burdens' and by Jesus himself.

All this has strong implications as we come to the sixth chapter of Ephesians. I struggle with the overt militarism of the 'whole armour of God' passage (6:10–20), believing that it is at odds with the previous submission, or 'yieldedness', imagery. This further suggests the multi-authorship of Ephesians. Yet before Tychicus is commended as a co-worker to the Ephesian church, there is a clear exhortation to continual and ongoing prayer (6:18). To pray on every occasion, as instructed, is to create a whole new lifestyle of prayer. Obviously, to pray continually for others' needs would be exhausting – and wrong. We have to find ourselves released into a can-do life of prayer, involving adoration, praise, thanksgiving, contemplation, meditation and so on, as well as simply praying for others.

The problem for many Christians is that we were captured into a particular kind of church, which probably focused on one or two ways of praying – rather than releasing us into a place where we could experience diversity and space. A whole new habitat of prayer.

Dwelling in a 'habitat of prayer'

As someone involved elsewhere with the ethical debates of zoo management and wildlife conservation, I am very much aware of the changes of the past half-century. Gone are the neo-Victorian barren cages and aviaries; even the word 'enclosure' is used much less in favour of 'habitat'. Often involving mixed species, the habitat contains a natural world of living plants and substrates and not a bland concrete reconstruction. In reputable zoos, animals no longer just exist, they dwell, live and breed in them; if they cannot thrive, they should not be kept.

So it is in the spiritual life. We need to dwell and thrive in a 'habitat of prayer'. We need to draw our resources for prayer from the Trinitarian orthodoxy from an ecumenical breadth. Why shouldn't a Baptist or Pentecostal use prayer drawn from an Anglican prayer book or the lives of the saints? Why should Roman Catholics not be encouraged to say extemporary prayers? Why should Christians be confined to the cages of our past separatism? The substrate of our individual spirituality needs to be a living reality, which encourages growth and vitality.

This is how the early church of the first few centuries grew. Why not again? The church has to recover being a 'habitat of prayer'. The church historian Alan Kreider makes this point in his excellent monograph *The Patient Ferment of the Early Church* (2016), where he utilises the '*habitus* thinking' of the contemporary sociologist Pierre Bourdieu. The *habitus* is not just the accepted theory or substrate of ideas but the decisive pattern of living behaviour or practice, arising from and interacting with the underlying philosophy. Kreider and his wife, Eleanor, a liturgist, pastor and musician, are renowned globally as Mennonite Christian educators. In a tribute to their lifelong shared ministry, a book of over 40 appreciative essays (what academics call a *festschrift*) was published, called *Forming Christian Habits in Post-Christendom*.[5]

Forming Christian habits is exactly what dwelling in a 'habitat of prayer' must mean. All of us, not just our teachers and denominational leaders, must have developed habits which can be recognised by others. I have to work hard at tilling my vegetable garden in order to grow crops that others recognise and want to eat. So it is with our prayers: we must work hard to enrich the habitat in which others recognise the credibility of our prayer lives. This is ever more necessary in our present age of multiculturalism, increasing secularism and personal agnosticism. No wonder the labels 'post-Christendom' and 'post-Christian' are becoming more common.

The prayers of the church's tradition

Apart from the prayers revealed in the Bible, the rich history of the church has produced prayers which are drawn into common parlance. Fifty years ago, at our grammar school's daily quasi-religious assembly, we recited the prayer of St Ignatius on Tuesday ('Teach us O Lord to serve thee as thou deservest') and the prayer of St Francis ('Make me a channel of your peace') on Friday, every week. When I questioned both that recitation style and the juxtaposition of a soldier-turned-Jesuit's devotions with the peace-making, nature-loving habit of an earlier saint, the head teacher was not impressed. But I still believe that our prayer lives reveal what kind of Christians we are. How do you ensure that the habit of prayer is not mere repetition or recitation?

From the heart of both the Christian creeds and academic theology comes the important (Latin) principle of *lex orandi, lex credendi* – 'we pray what we believe'. Although this has been part of the Western Roman Catholic and Eastern Orthodox teaching for centuries and though the Protestant Reformation re-established its centrality, it was the Methodist theologian Geoffrey Wainwright, in his 1980 *Doxology* that forced UK free churches to wrestle afresh with this concept. If we pray what we believe, what does your prayer life say about your faith?

Until AD1054, the Western (later Roman Catholic) and Eastern (later Orthodox) Church was as one, with regional patriarchs and indigenous communities, such as the various strands of the Celtic Church. One of the most beautiful prayers to teach new, adult Christians is 'the Jesus Prayer' which comes from that Orthodox tradition. Its six words are: 'Lord Jesus, have mercy on me.' A later addition to it were the words 'a sinner'.

The Jesus Prayer was intended to be said silently while breathing in, then reflected upon while slowly breathing out. Its simple recognition is that we need the forgiveness and mercy of Jesus as we acknowledge our own shortcomings in failing to live up to Jesus' standards. It is akin to those daily moments of reflection when we recognise the forbearance of our partner or spouse in the face of our own shortcomings. How much more, then, do we realise our shortcomings and failures when confronted with the invitation and glory of God revealed in Jesus? No wonder that 'the Jesus Prayer' is part of my daily life as I still my heart for prayer.

As I write this, close to my desk are some books of prayers written by Brother Roger of Taizé, Celtic-styled and Anabaptist-flavoured Christians as well as by those recognised as saints. There is also a shelf of historic and contemporary prayer books, drawn from across the ecumenical spectrum. During my life, these have become woven together to help create the fabric of my prayer life. Increasingly, I am rediscovering that the grace of many traditional prayers underpins the patterns and habits of mission now.

I have been greatly blessed that much of my ministry coincided with an explosion of Christian paperback publishing, which has subsided since the new millennium. A great many books of prayer and books about prayer were published, and were affordable, during that boom period. Many of these books are now appearing in charity shops or second-hand sales, so we all can benefit from them. It is quite simple to build up a small yet orthodox collection about the life of prayer, and I encourage you to do so. A dozen or more such paperback books would still only take up a small amount of shelf space.

Let me offer some guidelines, however, so that you buy good, orthodox material rather than those from the crackpots. Look at what the writer does: are they a bishop or denominational leader? Does the book say they are the 'vicar of x' or other kind of minister or parish priest? Does the content use Christian language which you can understand and have some poetic resonance when you read the prayers within it? Are they from known contemporary Christian communities, such as Taizé, Iona, Northumbria and so on, or from one of the historic orders, such as the Franciscans or Benedictines. The important thing is to discover which and whose forms of prayer help you develop that everyday *habitus* of prayer, then build from that. You can always donate the less helpful books back to the charity shop.

Developing our life of prayer

A few years ago I went on a retreat as a participant. I had recently retired from full-time ministry (for health reasons) and had begun writing afresh for publication. I wanted to give my own life a spiritual check-up. In the opening session, I was surprised at how many of the other participants had a similar aim or were also experiencing a time of transition in their personal life. As many of us were former ministers, Christian educators or some other kind of church professional, that initial candour marked the enrichment of our time together.

Early on, a former nun, Sister Brigid, led us through thinking about our lives *as* prayer not just lives of prayer. She told how she always sat quietly on her daily bus journey, hands clasped on her lap, eyes virtually closed, with a plain headscarf on, and received many 'Say one for me, sister' comments. She also set some helpful spiritual exercises, which our group reviewed towards the end of the week. All of this echoed and emphasised Kreider's '*habitus* of prayer'.

Previously, as a busy pastor, my prayer life was limited to when I was locked away in my study, or at our parish's few midweek prayer meetings and Sunday services, or at the bedsides of the sick and dying. I learned so much from Sister Brigid, who before her recent death kindly gave me permission to use her notes in my own conference and retreats ministry. Life *is* prayer – the very breathing of the Jesus Prayer fulfils in every sense its can-do action of inspiration.

I tell you all this because wherever we are on the spectrum of learning about prayer, it is never complete. We always have more to learn and experience if both our own prayer life and our empathy with others, in understanding their needs and prayer requests, are to deepen and grow. We learn by sharing the insights from others' journeys in the common life of our discipleship. All this is necessary if our mission efforts are to share that integrity too.

Towards a greater understanding of intercession

Jesus' first disciples all learned something of prayer from the Galilean synagogues. Yet they still knew that they could not pray like Jesus. Hence their request, 'Lord, teach us to pray.'

Jesus taught them a prayer, which the later church kept in its shorthand scriptural form and called the Lord's Prayer. Some of us say it privately every day or in company with a few others in our local parish church. Others use it with a home-based discipleship group as a prayer of intent, sometimes standing and holding hands, sometimes with eyes open, slowly and deliberately looking around as we say the words together. Some of us only use it together congregationally as we gather Sunday-by-Sunday. Whatever our practice, its use unites us with the whole Jesus-shaped community down through the ages.

While its opening phrases, 'Father in heaven, your name be honoured, your reign come', tell of adoration and praise, there is little intercession for others. Personal petition is both conditional and immediate: 'forgive us as we forgive others' and 'give us today (just) our daily bread', as well as the cry not to be tested beyond our human endurance. The Lord's Prayer ends with the affirmation of the ongoing glory of God: 'For yours is the reign, the power, the glory – forever!' This prayer is *the* prayer of our mutual and shared purpose of our discipleship. It is an outspoken commitment to gathering around Jesus' words and ways, to further the reign of God throughout eternity. It is the prayer of the Christian common life. John Dominic Crossan, the New Testament theologian, describes it as the prayer of 'distributive justice', the marker prayer of Jesus' egalitarian community.[6] *Lex orandi, lex credendi*

Therefore, all other prayer becomes secondary to that primary commitment to the common life which we share in Jesus. None of this belittles the place of intercession, for we know that this was also part of Jesus' own prayer life – think of his prayer for the entombed Lazarus and over a few loaves and fishes when surrounded by masses of hungry people.

While we must allow prayer to permeate our being, we have to ensure and recognise how Jesus' teaching (in his words, works and ways) is at its core. Intercession is no mere window dressing nor appendage to our central communal prayer life, affirmed by our individual and corporate saying of the Lord's Prayer. Intercession is a personal willingness to be so affected by the needs of others that we bring that need to the God-we-know-in-Jesus that we may share in the heart of God's response to that particular need. None of this precludes the divine prompting of the Spirit to respond miraculously or via human intervention to that particular need.

Therefore, we are not absolved from personal intercessory prayer. Some years ago, I was the facilitator for a regular, residential ecumenical gathering of clergy. During a session on prayer, one of our number said this: 'We used to pray for hardly anybody, so nobody got well or found their needs met, then we started regular intercessions and some of our prayers were answered, now we pray as much as we can for others and even more get healed or whatever.' That encouraged many of our congregations to take seriously God's invitation to be more truly intercessors.

As our faith matures and deepens, each of us must find ways to express how our prayer and spirituality is vital to our faith. It was

St Francis of Assisi who exhorted his followers with 'Share the gospel [that is, good news]. If necessary, use words.' He was right. Prayer, faith and spirituality must become so much part of the fabric of our lives, that our words become the supplementary emphases to our attitudes and actions in everyday life.

Group discussion questions

1 How do you ensure that the habit of prayer is not mere repetition or recitation, particularly when we draw from resources across the Christian tradition?

2 What particular resources that you use to help your prayers would you recommend?

3 Which line or part of the Lord's Prayer causes you to stop in your tracks whenever you say it?

7

Be still and know

The disciples asked Jesus 'teach us to pray' (Luke 11:1). Whatever else they recognised about Jesus, they knew him to be a man of prayer, even a master of prayer. It is natural to learn from those with greater facility in a particular skill or practice.

Every time I move house, as I did last year, I thank God for the carpentry skills that I learned from my dad and my school woodwork teachers, so that I can build kitchen cupboards and bookshelves. My dad was a pastor who had learned from the master carpenter to pray, and he did so publicly Sunday by Sunday among those who helped nurture me in faith. Dad was out busily pastoring each evening so it was my mum who taught me as a child how to pray each night: that practice remains with me over 60 years later!

We all need to learn to pray. The two preceding chapters demonstrated why, on the assumption that you already knew how. I have delayed this section until now to help us all realise how often we assume that others just understand what prayer is and how to do it. Do not feel guilty if you too made those assumptions, but be encouraged that we can review what and how we and our Jesus-shaped communities need to address this.

Praying for beginners

Churches, congregations, Jesus-shaped communities – whatever we call them – need to become schools of prayer if they are to truly become springboards for mission. As a pastor, I have always run my believers' baptismal classes together with our annual confirmation classes, as this is the personal, mature declaration of 'Jesus as Lord' by each individual, with the activist promise to follow him and his teaching. Part of that habit, even *habitus*, is to enable a personal practice of prayer to mature. As part of that exploration, I and a couple of elders would lead sessions to openly explore people's questions as well as different aspects of prayer, which we have been reviewing in these chapters. We used to create a buddy system for each new Christian, but I have to admit that recent child protection and vulnerable adult legislation now makes me wary of advocating such one-to-one practice.

Teaching people to pray, alongside how to read the Bible creatively, is both a privilege and a responsibility. I grew up in an Anabaptist-style conference of churches with weekly communion, only believers' baptism, regular meals in home groups and 'the prayers of the church'. This latter practice occurred during congregational worship, when anyone, young or old, female or male, could publicly lead the whole congregation in prayer. Often this was intercession but frequently included thanksgiving or adoration. We learned how to pray by listening to a rich diversity of others' prayers. We may have begun with one-liners: 'Gracious God, today, we pray for the victims of the earthquake in... Please show us how we can begin to help them in their need. In Jesus' name.' The resounding 'Amen' around you made you aware that your voice was part of the 'prayers of the church'. This engendered a can-do and participative approach in the practice of discipleship and mission across our community of faith.

I have Anglican friends who were brought up to learn the set prayers of the liturgy and are now raising their children to learn the same so that they can join in even if they cannot yet read. In a manner similar to my own upbringing, the church's prayers become woven into the fabric of their lives. Now that few schools, other than those that are church-sponsored, hold daily Christian assemblies, it becomes the responsibility of parents and Jesus-shaped communities to help people assimilate a practice of prayer from their youngest days.

When I was a minister in Kent, the owner of my local Christian bookshop gave me a book, suggesting I prayerfully consider it, given the fact that several of my congregation visited his store looking for prayer manuals. That book was Bill Hybels' *Too Busy Not to Pray* and it was a timely intervention into my ministry. We began separate *Too Busy Not to Pray* groups for men and women; both were fully subscribed within hours of publicising them. Two of our elders led the midweek women's group, several times over, while I led each of the four successive men's groups on Saturday mornings over breakfast. The problem was quickly apparent.

Despite many of these groups' participants being mature Christians, they all wanted refreshing teaching to help them reinvigorate their daily prayer lives amid a weight of competing demands. As we shared candidly together, they too had made assumptions about prayer and how it works. The congregation underwent some clear spiritual renewal as a result and I learned that even those with mature faith need and want to go back to basics to deepen their spirituality. Do you need to do that, too?

Lectio divina

Lectio divina is the practice of disciplined spiritual reading. Historically, it has two patterns. The first is corporate, often in monastic communities when some piece of acknowledged spiritual writing is read aloud during a meal or assembly, while the listeners eat and reflect silently. The second is individual, when the reader will silently read and reread the same chapter of a spiritual classic, then reflect upon it for several days before either discussing it with their spiritual director or pastor or going on to the next chapter, repeating the same process. Both methods can also use biblical reading in the same way.

Corporately, the reading is often drawn from the writings of the lives of the saints or those of the order's founder, such as St Benedict,

St Francis or Brother Roger. These can also be used individually, but often the English mystics, such as Julian of Norwich or Richard Rolle, or other writers, such as Richard Baxter, John Henry Newman, Dietrich Bonhoeffer or Sara Maitland, have their importance for an individual's spiritual challenge and development. The important thing when reading without guidance is to widen your horizons to orthodox and historic writers; cathedral bookshops are often a good source of such breadth.

The purpose of *lectio divina* is to engage the mind into thought and reflection about the life of the faithful. Some describe this as simply an intellectual practice, yet agree it becomes an ideal preparation for contemplation and meditation. Note the contrast with the writings of *devotio moderna*, such as à Kempis' *The Imitation of Christ*.

When leading church weekends for adults, I often suggest using *lectio divina* at Saturday lunchtime (with a well-chosen reading) to help engage people with its practice. I was happily surprised when staying in a Bruderhof community to find they also practised *lectio divina* at lunchtimes, with all ages present. At times I will play a CD of plainsong or worship from a historic monastery or from Taizé or the Northumbria Community, using their written words in place of a reading. But I still have my shelves of spiritual readers. The key part of the practice is active engagement with it: this is not book-at-bedtime stuff. It is about engaging with the considered reflection of someone whose faith journey has much to teach your own. How can *lectio divina* enrich your spiritual life?

Practising the presence of God

When I have travelled abroad, I have become quickly aware of how easily others in predominantly non-Christian cultures accept the practice of prayer. The daily calls to prayer from minarets in Muslim countries became a familiar sound. In India, the ubiquitous imagery of the pantheon of Hindu gods, even on bus-station walls, told of faith in the public square. In the Himalayas, Japan and South-East Asia, the prevalence of Buddhist temples, public prayer wheels and contemplative pilgrim pathways spoke of nations at ease with shared spiritualities and prayer.

We only need to see the crowds gathering outside British mosques or *musalla* (prayer rooms) on Fridays or gurdwaras on Saturdays to realise how much prayer is not a cultural matter but a vibrant natural expression of faith. This is in sharp contrast to the declining number of those frequently attending Christian worship in these same islands. Agnostic Britain is becoming more secular in its thinking, leading to an increasing number of questions about the relevance of prayer. How often in the British press do we read stories of new country dwellers objecting to the Sunday morning disturbance of church bells? Many now find even such a traditional 'call to prayer' a nuisance, but perhaps these folk also object to the smell of muck-spreading or the sound of combine harvesters working through the night – and are really out of touch with the fabric of real life.

While there is delight and often noise in Messy Church, at its heart is the aim to enable participants to build a living relationship with Jesus. I have been privileged to lead quiet days for Messy Church, FoodBank and soup-kitchen volunteers, when we always need to remind ourselves that these ministries must exude the calm, prayerful presence of the risen Christ just as much as those busy moments of putting food into hands. Often when speaking at clergy retreats or study weeks, a common concern is how the busyness of parish ministry puts the calmness of a practice of prayer under pressure.

Over many years, I have found deep wells of prayerful resource in the prayers of Celtic Christianity, whether those written in today's idiom or those collected from the borderlands in preceding centuries. Each prayer is often written to be slowly and repeatedly said as we go about mundane and everyday tasks, whether it is lighting the woodstove, milking the cow or preparing food to share.

Some of those prayers are simply adoration and thanksgiving as we still our heart to reflect with their silently uttered words on the gift of the Trinity or a sunrise, to acknowledge God's overwhelming faithfulness. This is about prayer and spirituality for every Christian in any and every walk of life.

Several years ago, I stayed in a New Age pagan commune for nearly a week as part of a sabbatical journey. The subject I was questioned about most was my practice of prayer. I shared a guest room, so I would disappear to a field shelter at the far side of the vegetable patch to pray quietly and alone. 'What are you doing?' 'Why?' But my co-residents were more interested in what it meant to have a 'practice of prayer'. We each need to question ourselves about whether our friends, family and contacts recognise us as people of prayer.

Teaching neighbours to 'be still and know'

As in that commune, we may not be able to shut the door and pray privately. However, we need to live and act as people of prayer if our neighbours and friends are to come to view our faith as having integrity. How we talk about our belief in God's healing ministry will determine whether others trust us with their concerns and fears for our intercessions.

In Chapter 5, we looked briefly at the injunction in Psalm 46 to 'Be still and know that I am God'. At its outset this psalm affirms that 'God is our refuge and strength, a very present help in trouble' (v. 1). The very fact that God is God and will always be a 'present help' is vital as we offer intercessory prayer for our neighbours. We are demonstrating that we live with the reality of God's existence and help. In doing that, we affirm that prayer is not made in our own strength but that of God. We just have to 'be still and know' that God is God.

So it is that our prayer life and our calm contemplation of the world's ills can speak to friends and neighbours that our trust is in God alone.

They can lean on our faith and allow us to pray in the stillness for their needs. As they come to know that we are faithfully concerned for them and that we will intercede in prayer for them, so they can know they are as important to God as we are.

This is mission. We are helping them through our everyday lives of prayer to recognise and trust our reliance on the reign of God. As they see our quiet joy in God's answers to our prayers, whether for themselves or others, they will begin to accept that God is reigning over the issues of their lives too. Then the gospel really does become good news – as we will see in the next section, 'Tell'.

Contemplation and meditation

Patterns of contemplation can be personally developed; the practice of meditation needs to be taught. Both add their essential vitality to a deepening and mature Christian faith. As we gradually gather small eat-pray-tell groups from our neighbourhood, we have to be spiritually mature enough to know when to just listen, when to halt someone's unethical thinking and when to admit you need to reflect with another Christian leader about what is being said. In recognising your own practice of prayer, your guest should accept advocacy in this, without withdrawing from future invitations. What I am saying is that alongside your hospitality, you must also be strengthening your prayer life.

Contemplation and *lectio divina* often walk hand-in-hand. Our ability to reflect deeply upon matters of faith will be enriched by the greater understanding of others. So it is often worth collecting inexpensive paperback editions of those works which have spoken deeply to you over a matter of years. Then as others grow to trust you and your faith judgements, those who enjoy reading can be helped on their journey by borrowing a suitable book, with the sage advice to read it slowly, taking a few days between each chapter. Contemplation is an acquired gift that broadens as we exercise it, but initially we can be best served by having a book or an icon as a focus for our contemplation rather than snoozing at the sunset.

The practice of meditation requires time, a good teacher and the opportunity to meditate daily in a calm environment. Like a child learning to ride a bike, we need to gain our balance before we can let go of the external stabilisers to meditate well and alone. Initially we have to learn the mechanics of relaxation and breathing, to aid our greater concentration on that which is Other (i.e. God). We also have to be taught and instil the personal discipline of keeping our minds from wandering. My good friend Father Allan Armstrong, the writer and prior of a small contemplative order, has helped hone my meditation practice over recent years – 40 years after undergraduate Buddhist friends suggested it might be a good practice to acquire. I am beginning to understand more of what it means to have a lifetime of prayer.

A daily quiet time

Some years ago, there was a plethora of helpful teaching and material, particularly from evangelicals, about the need to create and maintain a daily personal quiet time. Even if we lack sufficient time to formally meditate or contemplate, we need such a daily quiet time.

In commuter-belt Kent, I was often asked about this by uber-busy people, particularly those with families. They often had large houses, good salaries and spacious kitchen-diners. I used to advocate having a particular breakfast-bar stool which individuals would only sit on while relishing their quiet time. One family took this up in earnest: the husband got up early for half an hour of Bible study and prayer before leaving for his daily London-bound train; his wife used the same stool and the quiet of the house after the school run. Later, their teenage son adopted the same routine with his wide window-ledge at university. Several months after sharing this at a conference,

I received a letter from a woman who after hearing me, bought a bar stool from a charity shop for her spare bedroom and transformed her daily prayer life – simply by sitting on it to pray every day!

For some years, until my knees became arthritic, I used a Taizé-style prayer stool to kneel and pray on my study floor. Simply the change from my desk chair took away the distraction of adjacent paperwork, open books or the window before me. Then, I often sat on the crook of my stairs, with a candle lantern on the window-ledge and a cross high on the wall. Now because of more discipline and learning about meditation, I can use a straight-back chair at the dining table, while the house is quiet. Depending upon my day's work, I might have my opened Bible or prayer book or a lit candle as a focus on the table in front of me, but my need to pray hardly wavers and the blessing of those devotional moments remains vital.

Some years ago, there was a popular bumper sticker which read 'Seven days without prayer make one weak'. It still is true. Our task as Jesus' followers is to adopt his prayerful life and help others to do the same. At the most basic level, if we offer to pray for others, we need to be able to do just that, trusting that we too have learned how to enter into the rich presence of God on behalf of others.

Group discussion questions

1   What key lesson can you share from your own practice of prayer?

2   How much do we understand ourselves to be part of a 'community of prayer' rather than a 'congregation'?

3   What circumstance (i.e. time of day, space, resources, etc.) helps us most fully to engage in recognising the presence of God as we pray?

Tell

8

There is good news!

At the end of Jesus' earthly ministry, just before he ascended into heaven, Matthew reports Jesus' final instructions to his followers: 'Go therefore and make disciples of all nations, baptizing them in the name of the Father and of the Son and of the Holy Spirit, and teaching them to obey everything that I have commanded you' (Matthew 28:19–20a). This multiple instruction is known as the great commission.

While I do not intend to resolve the arguments between biblical commentators as to whether these verses are Jesus' own words or those of the early church or a later liturgical interpolation, it is important to note Jesus' all-encompassing emphases – 'all' and 'everything' – *remain* in these instructions. The task of Jesus' ongoing followers, including you and me, is to play our part in fulfilling the great commission. Our role includes 'telling' the good news, enabling individual change – for this is what personal salvation entails.

Jesus' eat-pray-tell mission's purpose is to enable each person to acknowledge that the reign of God is here and now, and then turn around their life to live out that reign. The Greek word for conversion is *metanoia*, which means 'turning around'. People will only do this when they acknowledge that what is being offered to them is good news.

Lesslie Newbigin, the missionary bishop, wrote that 'Jesus entrusted to his community the responsibility of interpreting all that concerned himself and promised that as his community went out into all the nations, with their varying languages and cultures, they would be led into the fullness of the truth.'[7]

What do we tell?

My large *Collins English Dictionary* defines 'gospel' as 'the story of Christ's life and teaching as narrated in the Gospels' and 'the good news of salvation in Jesus Christ', among several further definitions. Unless Christians tell the story from their faith-full perspective, the good news will be relegated to secular educationalists' version of the first definition, with the second definition's emphasis upon good news and salvation being dropped.

We must tell the good news of Jesus in both word and deed. Without that, the church is one generation from extinction – ours! We have good news to tell.

Several house-moves ago, I arrived in a neighbourhood with quite an anti-social resident. Both his and his teenage children's loud, public use of bad language, their ill-trained dogs, noisy late-night visitors and derelict vehicles upset many of us. I shared this situation with a new colleague, who volunteered his wife's services as a local district nurse to help us. Suitably uniformed, she approached the offender's front door and quietly asked to have a discussion with him. After his initial Anglo-Saxon outburst, she repeated her request and was invited in for a cup of tea. She explained that the dog mess was a health hazard to young children, that the bad language was affecting the 'nerves of the older people' because they were frightened of the family and so on. The difficult neighbour protested 'Why didn't anyone tell me?', but got rid of the old cars, disciplined his children, cleaned up his own language and cleaned up after his dogs. The neighbours began talking with them and our street's atmosphere changed for the better. You will have to decide how many steps he took towards redemption, but someone had to tell him that change was necessary. Without that, he could not turn around from his belligerence and bad behaviour towards becoming a better neighbour.

The gospel of Jesus causes change in many dynamic ways.

Just like that anti-social neighbour, folk need to be told how and why to change their lives in Jesus' way. We can no longer assume the 'everyone goes to Sunday school' approach or that they have heard the good news of Jesus' invitation.

For nearly 40 years, we have been singing a mission-oriented hymn which asks its singers to think 'how shall they call if they have never heard the gracious invitation of the Lord'. In today's secularising world, Christians must find a way of sharing that gracious invitation of the Lord. But we can only speak with people when they are ready to listen, and have cause and occasion to do so. Eat, pray, tell gives that opportunity because in accepting the invitation to share a meal, people are expressing a willingness to receive hospitality and to enter into *appropriate* conversation.

That qualifier is important. We must learn to temper our enthusiasm with appropriate restraint. We should not spill out a heavy version of Jesus' good news and demand immediate commitment during our first gathering together. One of the best maxims, which an itinerant evangelist gave me, is that you cannot drive a ten-ton message over a one-ton relationship.

Making the good news relevant again

It was Dean Inge of St Paul's Cathedral who reputedly once said, 'The church which marries itself to the spirit of the age, will be a widow in the next.' How true that has been proved. Let me offer two simple examples from the 1960s:

- When the BBC screened their original adaptation of *The Forsyte Saga* on Sunday evenings, many congregations dwindled and some churches closed their evening services, denying corporate worship to some who never returned. A few churches bought big screens and tried to compete by showing films of faith, testimony and some very American documentaries to attract a congregation.

But those electronic churches failed to move with the increasingly fast technological changes and now have mainly gone.

- Other churches tried to respond to the then popular 'God is dead' discussion by advancing secular theologies with arid worship and intellectual debates, instead of vibrant prayer and shared biblical exploration of Jesus' call to be community. They, too, failed.

It is my contention that those churches which remained faithful to evolving patterns of community, enlivening prayer, meditative silence and rich liturgy and which encouraged their fellowship to mark out Sundays differently from Monday to Saturday lived well enough to thrive another day. Those marks of 'pray' and 'eat' are still part of Jesus' mission today.

For nearly a year, while the denomination reappraised local pastorates, I served as oversight minister to a small congregation in a predominantly retired dormitory community, some distance from my home. I was only scheduled to lead Sunday worship once each month, attend two evening meetings per month and offer an afternoon per week to visit their sick, lead the women's meeting or take funerals. Such a minimal time commitment to help lead a local congregation into renewal, but it is what many busy vicars have to cope with in united benefices or multi-congregation pastorates.

Before my second Sunday there, I encouraged two of the elders to each host Sunday lunch for a different group of parishioners. I joined one group for sherry and the main course and dashed to the other for dessert and coffee. My sermon that morning had been built around Jesus-shaped eating and the call to hospitality. During that sermon I encouraged the congregation to begin gathering for Sunday lunch in each other's homes. They did – and the church grew during my year with them, as did my waistline, as well as the number of lunch hosts. Each host always took the initiative to invite a non-churchgoing neighbour or two as well. In this pattern of 'loving their neighbours', they relearned how to build Christian community.

Now I do realise that in many places the name of Jesus has simply become an expletive, and not a byword for an exciting community. The church in its myriad forms has much work to do in restoring the honour of the name and life-changing call of Jesus. So we have to begin where people are – and be prepared to begin again. Much of that is to do with us personally and how we behave and respond to others. We never get a second chance to make that first impression.

We also have to be clear about the interplay between gospel and culture. There are strong arguments from history that the church was at its most successful when its life and teaching engaged and challenged that of the surrounding culture. We only need think of the church before Constantine to recognise this. Or, despite the fact that most Britons simply credit only Wilberforce, the importance of the role of the church across Britain in advancing legislation to abolish slavery shows how effective countercultural activism can be. Or, in our generation, our response to the many discussions about human sexuality can demonstrate how *we* understand both the interplay between gospel and culture as well as the role of the Bible in society. Every intelligent Christian needs to discover a couple of sentences (comfortably for them) about how the Bible and cultural issues can become conversation partners to help answer the confrontational questions about issues facing society.

We have to meet people how and where they are. Then, if we are to communicate the gospel to them, we have to build the kind of relationship which keeps conversation and opportunities alive. By now, you may not need to be reminded that one of the best ways to do this is by eating together. It *might* not matter whether that is on the wall outside the fish-and-chip shop or at a supper party in your home, but grace, courtesy and a willingness to listen to others can build a lot of bridges.

A couple of Christian friends of mine moved to Milton Keynes. After they had settled in, they regularly invited a neighbouring non-Christian couple for supper, roughly once a month. On a few occasions, they invited another Christian couple to join them but kept the conversation to the issues of the day. After a year they began inviting another newly arrived non-Christian couple each month, and they all became friends. In the third year, they invited another couple and regularly smiled when the first couple of invitees used to offer Christian perspectives into the conversation. That first couple then began hosting their own monthly supper party and attending one of the local churches. The pattern repeated itself until my friends had to move because of the husband's advancing terminal illness. Sometimes we have to take a long-term, even a lifetime view, over our participation in sharing Jesus' good news.

We must find a way to create ice-breaking conversation that is authentic and not contrived. It must involve our individual story, too, or it becomes irrelevant. Let me offer this example. There are several pictures, large and small, in my home as well as inexpensive *objets d'art*, which often intrigue new visitors. One is a wall-mounted plate from Israel, with the word 'shalom' in Hebrew and English within its glaze. Another is a slate Celtic cross from Iona. There is a Troika-styled pottery table lamp, given to me by American Mennonites as well as another gift from North Africa of a picture of Noah's ark upon a turbulent sea. Each say something of my life's Christian narrative and can be conversationally recounted in response to others' interest. So as friends and neighbours, old and new, gather for summer barbecues, seasonal buffets and Christmas drinks, there is a story to share, which always involves the good news of life in Jesus' community.

'The year of the Lord's favour'

In a previous book, *Shalom: The Jesus Manifesto*, I recounted how we used the Lukan version of Isaiah's proclamation of the 'year of the Lord's favour' (Luke 4:18–19) as the corporately spoken congregational call to worship at my launch service for an inner-city ministry in Leeds.

There, I was to work with a few often-struggling congregations, some local inner-city home-based groups and ecumenical mission initiatives. Together, we were to help the United Reformed Church in Yorkshire rethink the challenge of urban mission. That story, its challenges and our human frailties have not nearly been documented enough. But together we all learned more of the truth about the 'year of the Lord's favour'. While Sunday by Sunday we redeveloped our patterns of multi-voiced worship and ways of gathering, across all our groups each week we offered three topics or people's names for daily personal prayer (one of our Saturday volunteers phoned through the three concerns to every group each week). We tried to ensure that each of our groups, whether engaged in telling the Jesus-story or serving neighbourhood groups, could share food together, even if only tea and home-made cake. The year of the Lord's favour meant that some of those who were blind to the church's purpose saw it differently; some who had been deaf to Jesus' message began to hear; some who had been captive to the oppression of long-term illness, alcoholism or unemployment found liberation in volunteering or participating in one or other of our activist groups. This was good news as Jesus intended, and as Isaiah had prophesied nearly a millennium before that.

What we have to recognise is that we must enable the gospel to speak at the level and into the culture and neighbourhood of those whom we are trying to offer the good news of Jesus to. What I mean, my brothers and sisters, is this (to quote Paul, the missionary church planter):

- **Level**: we have to recognise that traditional overseas missions did not work with an Alpha mentality of ensuring everyone had a Bible and inviting them to discuss the text. It began with narrative (i.e. telling the story), prayer, healings and sharing resources, such as food and skills. Eat, pray, tell is an easy way to offer participation at the right level for everyone, because we should not be pressuring people to conform in a particular way.

- **Culture:** we live within different cultures in 21st-century Britain. Just think cross-generationally: my adult children pick up the news electronically on the move at whatever time, whereas I prefer my morning newspaper and scheduled BBC Radio 4 news programmes. When I lived in Kent there was a dinner-party culture, whereas previously in Leeds and now in the West Country we are far more attuned to informal supper parties. How folks eat together – around a table or buffet style – tells us something about the culture in which we live, and how as hosts we need to make our guests feel comfortable (see page 21).

- **Neighbourhood:** for many years I lived in different inner-city areas, with predominantly terraced homes. The small rooms restricted numbers yet meant everyone shared in a single conversation. I have also lived on the edge of an 'arty' suburb, where open-plan living, fork suppers, floor cushions and a local pattern of conversations flowing in and out of the gathered group, meant we needed more Christians anonymously mingling in our eat-pray-tell meals to fulfil our purpose.

If we are to bring 'the year of the Lord's favour' into others' lives, we have to ensure that our eat-pray-tell meals work functionally, in their welcome and style as well as in maintaining the conversational direction we want.

'The year of the Lord's favour' has another implication for those whom we are seeking to draw into the Jesus-shaped community. They have to recognise that their participation and our eating together is a blessing to them. I sometimes have to remember that when I am washing up by hand at midnight, with an early start the next morning. We need to quickly encourage that group to become a proto(type)-community together; not by naming it but just by relationally building human links, helping each other in a practical task, from lending tools or books to offering time and so on. Our group once spent a whole Saturday helping the latest invitee couple clear the badly overgrown garden of their new house. That couple went on to become Christians; she still serves as a Congregational Church deacon and he preaches regularly. Serving others brings blessing – and often faith.

The integrity of the messenger

This subheading says it all. To use an old phrase, we have to practice what we preach. We need to be transparent when questioned about who we are and why people have been invited. We need honestly to say that, as Christians, we want others to encounter us not as media-caricatured bigots but as human beings who have discovered the blessing of 'the year of the Lord's favour' as we have sought to follow the words and ways of Jesus.

Chaucer wrote a wonderful poem about a highly devoted parish priest who spent his time meeting the practical needs of those in his parish and ministered well to the sick and dying. The poem explicitly makes the point that his witness was that he practised what he later went on to preach. This affirms an eat-pray-tell progression in today's world: we share with people what they need before explaining why we do what we do.

Some of us find the support in that journey of faith by participating in the congregation of a traditional denomination, or perhaps in a fresh expression of Christian gathering or even a more informal home-based discipleship group. But the integrity of our mutual accountability to each other, to Jesus and the wider Christian community depends upon our faithfulness to the words and ways of Jesus. That means both word and deed if our eat-pray-tell group will facilitate others to share that faith journey.

Group discussion questions

1 What does the 'year of the Lord's favour' mean to me personally?

2 How do we work out a priority for which parts of a Jesus-shaped message are important or less so for the neighbourhood around us?

3 What kind of support would *you* need from this group, or your wider Christian context, to share the gospel of Jesus in an eat-pray-tell group?

9

Learning by experience

Both eat, pray, tell and the broader understanding of mission are transforming experiences. They are purposefully meant to change people's lives. Michael Green, an Anglican missiologist, wrote the following about congregational fellowship groups that had adopted first-century patterns of outreach:

> The informal atmosphere, the naturalness of meeting, the food, the conversations, the friendships, the joint activities all make it easy to move on and off spiritual topics, and help the new Christian to adjust to the new society of which he has become a member.[8]

Green was writing about congregational life several stages on from our initial guests in our eat-pray-tell strategy, but his encompassing checklist helps us realise that all these aspects contribute to the transforming grace of Jesus' words and ways.

The lessons from transformational mission

So far, I have written of my understanding of eat, pray, tell. However, as we journey onward through these final chapters, it will be important to recognise that it is not just my analysis and advocacy which underpins this strategy in developing the pattern of Jesus' disciples for our present age. Increasingly, I will include the voices and writings of others from across the world and across the Christian community.

Since the 1920s the church in Britain has moved at increasing speed from a central place in society towards the margins. In nearly all cities, the church has become marginalised. But most Christians' self-awareness, understanding of mission and theology of church has not undergone what US philosopher Thomas Kuhn called the necessary 'paradigm shift' in our thinking and activity to accommodate these changes. Such a shift is game-changing in our thinking and causes us to change strategies significantly.

Nearly every thinking church leader (over the age of 40) should have studied and utilised with colleagues a copy of David Bosch's *Transforming Mission: Paradigm shifts in the theology of mission*. Bosch wrote this large masterful, academic overview of how the church has (and has not) been coping with these societal and ecclesial changes during this past century. His thesis is very clear: our former structures have served well, but globally the church must learn again from newer initiatives and small laity-led groups if mission – sharing the gospel authentically – is to succeed in rapidly changing and increasingly multicultural societies. Bosch reminds us that mission is transformative and the sharing of the gospel must transform others' lives not just spiritually but also practically and socially. Eat, pray, tell is but one important way to ride well that necessary paradigm shift in our practice of mission, at a local neighbourhood level.

Mission in our neighbourhood

This whole book is about earthing eat, pray, tell in your own neighbourhood. As I said in the previous chapter, we have many issues to check and confront as we engage with the level, culture and neighbourhood of our own immediate areas.

Knowing the beat of our street is important in understanding our neighbours' rhythms of life. What are the key concerns? What gets us animated locally? These are often the things which begin the conversations with those who live around us. Suburbs and dormitory villages may have bucolic names but little sense of shared identity, as people often drive elsewhere to shop, go to school, work and so on. It may only be the gradually developing relationships with other neighbours that will forge a sense of common well-being. Any eat-pray-tell gathering needs to have worked beyond the mutual moan about a local issue or key concern (acknowledging these are important) before conversation can really turn towards friendship-building.

Mission in our neighbourhood is relational. For many years, I had tacked above my study noticeboard a battered postcard that read, 'Evangelism is one blind beggar telling another blind beggar where to find bread.' This was a quote from Daniel T. Niles, a Sri Lankan theologian whose ministry encompassed work with neighbourhood Methodist congregations and in the 1960s leading the evangelistic thinking of the World Council of Churches. Niles reminds us that the search for bread is eternal and that despite our blind spots God can use us to enable others to find God in Jesus for themselves. Even in our self-perceived weaknesses, our eat-pray-tell hosting can feed others in body and soul. Now that is good news, in every sense.

Bosch used to take some pleasure in reminding church leaders at their conferences that 'Laypersons are... the operational basis from which the *missio Dei* [Latin for 'mission of God'] proceeds... it is the community which is the primary bearer of mission.'[9]

The cross-cultural agenda

The gospel of Jesus is for *all* people, as his great commission tells us. This means that local gatherings of those who follow Jesus' words, works and ways should be diverse. Sociologists' term for this is heterogeneous. First-century congregations were diverse, and that diversity, with rich and poor, slave and free, Jew and Gentile, made them even more attractive to pagans and other outsiders.

Many local British congregations are homogeneous; that is, they are made up of the same type of people, in terms of race, class, occupation type and income level. Part of this is to do with what economists call our demographic geography, in that rich people live in a particular kind of neighbourhood, where poorer or unemployed folk cannot afford to live. Just looking at our own town, we can recognise where the artisans or students or professional types tend to live. Eat-pray-tell groups often work best with similarly minded people, who are not going to be daunted by our type of housing or the way we live or how our way of table fellowship works. I have friends whose postgraduate children successfully host eat-pray-tell groups in the student quarters of several cities.

Initially, we may be wise to have a homogeneous eat-pray-tell group and learn how to make that work, discipling others with an outward-looking vision. But at some stage, if we are serious about eat, pray, tell as our ongoing key mission strategy, it will become cross-cultural. Our guests may well be of a different race or background or lifestyle to our own. We must learn to accommodate them, their needs and their type of conversation and questions. We must remember that they are made in God's image too and our task is not to try to remake them in our image – as so many colonial-era missionaries tried to do overseas.

As our guests become more diverse and gradually become friends, teaching us on the way about life from their perspective, our lives become enriched by the prophetic community which God's Spirit is drawing together.

As Bosch says:

> It is a fellowship, a *koinonia* [Greek for 'fellowship'], which actualises God's love in its everyday life and in which justice and righteousness are made present and operative... It is the good news of God's love, incarnated in the witness of a community, for the sake of the world.[10]

This speaks of God's cross-cultural mission, from a South African writer born into an apartheid system whose calling made him a global theologian and a human rights activist in everyday life.

God's love transcends barriers and margins – it is cross-cultural, because it reveals the culture of the cross, where all things are reconciled through Jesus' death and resurrection.

'Do not judge, so that you may not be judged'

Part of that cross-cultural agenda is to know our own boundaries. I serve only vegetarian food when we host Jewish, Hindu and Muslim guests. I do not maintain a kosher kitchen (separating milk- and meat-based meal preparation), so it is better that I do not try, and risk offending Jewish guests. It also means that my vegetarian partner and I share the same food as our guests. My views about animal welfare, organic farming and slaughter are well-documented. Therefore, as I prefer not to serve either halal or kosher meat, offering vegetarian food to Muslim and Jewish guests compromises nobody.

In Britain today, there are many secular Jews and 'people of the book' Muslims who welcome hospitality and invitations from Christian hosts. But do not be offended by refused invitations; just be aware that you opened up a hand of friendship. Equally, listen to the advice of your pastor and elders, as well as your congregational policy, about eat-pray-tell invitations to others. There are plenty of lapsed Christians and non-believers in our neighbourhoods who could welcome your hospitality and friendship.

You need to understand your own prejudices and boundaries. That nice couple with almost-adult children across the road may have never married; they won't thank you for telling them that they are 'living in sin' (as my grandparents' generation might have done) and would probably (fairly) refuse all further invitations. Civil partnerships are an accepted part of UK life, so you need to work out whether you can cope with a guest bringing a same-sex partner *before* inviting them. Whatever our views, several church denominations in the UK will conduct marriages for gay couples, so we do the broader mission of Jesus' people (the church) a profound disservice if we are immediately condemnatory of same-sex relationships. Inclusivity is a mark of Jesus' gospel, but it may be a step too far for you now. Acknowledge it in prayer and in discussion with your elder.

It is not just issues of sexuality that can cause us problems. We need to understand with our co-host how we can rebuff graciously the privately expressed racist or sexist views of our guests, or blasphemy or bad language in their speech. We often use responses such as, 'As Christians, we find that difficult because we believe all people are equal in God's sight'; 'Please, can you tone down the language because…'; and 'We struggle with using "God" or "Jesus Christ" like that, because they are real for us, and to hear their names used like that, hurts us.' Often it can be better for a female co-host to begin that response, with clear support (not an embarrassed 'I agree') from the other host. This seems to create less confrontation.

In one of my first ministries, much gossip, even opprobrium, prevailed about a newly arrived male couple at the edge of our neighbourhood. There must have been only a ten-year age gap between these two very different-looking, quiet-living guys, with an innate closeness between them. At weekends, that bond was often witnessed by my parishioners across the local steak bar. A whole mythology built up around them and I was asked about 'those kind of people'. Finally, I dropped a note through their letterbox saying I was going to call upon them. Over coffee and jazz, they told me they were stepbrothers, and the older one had brought up the younger one after their father and the younger's mother had died together in an accident. Gradually we became friends. They were frequent guests for meals and accepted an invitation to speak together at my congregation's annual service for bereaved families. I like to think that it was my parishioners who, in learning their story, helped rebut and destroy much of the gossip about them in that community. So, our eat-pray-tell mealtime conversations must avoid allowing gossip to prevail.

As that story shows, not everything is as it sometimes seems. Jesus' injunction 'Do not judge, so that you may not be judged' (Matthew 7:1, in traditional paraphrase) needs to be a warning to us all, particularly when adopting an eat-pray-tell strategy. We need to allow our guests gradually to share their stories without condemnation.

'Soapbox out – serving is in'

Years ago, there was a pastor's widow in one of my congregations. She was a lovely person, hospitable to not just friends and neighbours but very supportive of me as a young minister. It transpired that she had been widowed just months before her husband's retirement. Bravely she had moved across the country to settle in an unknown town, midway between her adult children's homes.

After my first Sunday lunch with her, while drying up, she instructed me to be thorough in wiping any water from the empty treacle sponge tin. I soon discovered that she used these tins to make pies and Christmas cakes, which she delivered to the sick and frail elderly across our neighbourhood – and occasionally to a bachelor minister. After I had been somewhat combative in a Sunday sermon, she invited me round on Monday afternoon for tea and home-made cake. The thrust of her gentle critique was 'soapbox out – serving is in'. I spent the rest of my ministry learning that lesson, and I remain grateful to God for the friendship, appropriately sized food gifts, wise advice and service that she gave to me and many others.

The helpful Greek word *diakonia* means 'service'. The word was appropriated by the church to describe the role of one who serves, as we find in the biblical orders of ministry (e.g. 1 Timothy 3:8–10).

It is the root of the modern-day office of deacon that we find (albeit in very different ways) in Anglican, Baptist and parts of the New Church movement. It is noteworthy that two of the most popular contemporary worship songs are Graham Kendrick's 'The Servant King' and Richard Gillard's 'Brother, Sister, Let Me Serve You' – each with their varied references to *diakonia*. But service needs to be more than a matter of affirmation, but of commitment. Remember the Chaucer poem about the devoted priest who served his parishioners?

Eat, pray, tell is rooted in our desire to serve others for Jesus' sake.

Group discussion questions

1   What kind of neighbourhood do we live in? How homogenous or heterogeneous is it?

2   How and what would we feel restricted by in asking some of our neighbours to come for a meal, initially as a one-off, but hopefully on a regular (say, monthly) basis to get to know them?

3   Why are we sometimes hesitant to explore new patterns of mission strategy, such as eat, pray, tell?

10

Growing as a Jesus-shaped community

Over my years as a pastor, I have discovered that many people find it easier to read books about different types of Christian practice than to daily read the Bible, synthesising their interpretation with others' thinking into practical discipleship. Perhaps this is because many of those books offer fresh narrative thinking about the church. Islam may regard Christians as a fellow 'people of the book', but we are not. We are a community with a story, which does not require sacred text to be memorised and quoted every other moment for God's reign to be made apparent by the bearers of that story, who are also sharers of God's provision.

The decisive compass point for every Christian is the words, works and ways of Jesus. It is this that binds us together into new cross-cultural relationships and different forms of community. There is an old joke that a camel is a racehorse designed by a committee. The problem is that it might have been that same committee which sought to constrain the reign of God into a vessel called the church. Did they try and say this is how the church must look, as a living thing with a leg at each corner? I think they were too prescriptive and we live with a camel of a church, which has to lurch its way lopsidedly across the increasing desert of secularism. They might have forgotten the dynamic variety of the creatures of God's creation. Our cat dozing on a chair close by is very different from the wild boar in our region's forest or the elephant in the nearby zoo. All have four legs but very different lives and ways of being what their Creator intended.

The same is true of the Jesus-shaped community with his story. We may have some common attributes, but we are allowed to be diverse and have very different lives. We have to live out counter-culturally attuned lives as communities with that Jesus story, continually prepared to share it in ways accessible to us and non-confrontationally for our friends and neighbours. Eat-pray-tell, anyone?

The subversive gospel

What we must always remember is that pre-Christendom (that is, before Constantine and others made Christianity the official religion of the empire), Christianity was just a counterculture, holding radically different values to the surrounding pagan mainstream. The gospel was subversive – and it still is.

In the challenging book *Seven Words for the 21st Century*, which re-examines Jesus' last seven 'words' (phrases really) from the cross, Rowan Williams wrote:

> The cross is where the non-citizens are executed; it defines the fact, much thought about by the earliest Christians, that belonging with the God of Jesus is the opposite of being a citizen, someone with clear, publicly agreed rights and status. The 'rights' of the Christian are grounded in active relation with God and each other rather than the law of the state. And this is not simply a transition into a mildly utopian community alongside the state (as if coming to belong with Jesus were like joining CND or the Green Party); it is to invite the unwelcome fate of being written out of the story, having no meaning that the public sphere can grasp. This has nothing to do with any kind of commendation by the powerful to the powerless to accept their doubtless disagreeable lot. It is an observation that in a society where non-citizens can be painfully and fairly casually slaughtered, God is not a citizen; so that if we are to

be found where God is, we can't stay safely within our citizen's rights.[11]

This reminds us that Christian discipleship is not just comfortable home-counties Anglicanism, nor bright, cheery hymn-singing Methodism, nor happy-clappy worship, but it is commitment to the cross, words and ways of Jesus. Lest ire has overtaken you, let me remind you that the above analysis is from the former Archbishop of Canterbury, with his lifetime of scholarship and prayer, rather than this present radical Anabaptist.

Eat, pray, tell is a subversive strategy to enable conversation over many meals to enable both the questioning and retelling of Jesus' subversive words and ways. Just like the early Christians, our strategy must be like a patient ferment, allowing our guests to become acquainted, then friends, then fellow pilgrims on a journey which follows those words and ways of Jesus. As hosts, we have much to learn from our guests as, meal after meal, they teach us how to share that subversive gospel.

If that journey over time has any meaning, we will have learned that our prayers for them will mean standing alongside their needs. Often our resources, including time, may form parts of God's answer to those prayers. When I have a car and clear time in my diary, why am I petitioning God for someone to take Bloggs to the hospital? Whether it is taking them to a hospital appointment, or lending them our tools and books, or taking them a casserole if they are unwell, God uses us to help answer prayer. In this way, God builds us up into the new community and blurs the boundary between host and guest. Or in Williams' analysis, God uses that new community to blur all distinctions, such as 'powerful' and 'powerless', re-emphasising the egalitarian nature of the community which honours and accepts the reign of God. When Jesus told those first disciples to share the reign of God through eat, pray, tell, he was enabling the gospel's subversion to thrive.

Life together

'Strengthening distinctive Christian community is at once one of the most essential and the most formidable challenges the church faces in the world.' Thus wrote Rodney Clapp, a theologian and astute social commentator, in the final chapter of his *A Peculiar People*.[12] Peculiar? Yes, because it really means 'distinct' (from others) rather than its colloquial meaning of strange or odd. Clapp entitled his last chapter, 'The church as community of friends', which is the thesis of this book too, that we eat, pray, tell our way into building a community of friends, whom others see distinctly and increasingly to be Christian. Do you recall that couple from Milton Keynes (page 87)?

Since my late teens I have been fascinated by the life and writings of Dietrich Bonhoeffer, a pastor who was hanged by the Nazis just weeks before World War II ended. His challenging book *Life Together* is threaded through with lessons from the life of the radical, and illegal, Confessing Church's seminary at Finkenwalde. How the pastors there shared privations, risk, meals, prayer and learning underscores Rowan Williams' comment about the subversive gospel just as fully as Bonhoeffer's own martyrdom does. *Life Together* affirms the centrality of Jesus Christ and his reign in creating a new community in which love and service are the prevailing values. Eat-pray-tell groups are decisive in enabling others to share this common understanding in their own time and in their own language and culture. As hosts, we enable others to share in the ferment of those Jesus-shaped values.

For over half my adult life, I have been welcomed and increasingly affirmed by, and learned much from, Mennonite communities in Britain, mainland Europe and North America. In the US, one Mennonite couple, Richard and Lois Landis, moved to a new town in New Jersey, where they knew no one. So they would go to a fast-food restaurant and take their trays to other people's tables, asking to join them in conversation about the area. Gradually they built friendships from which a community of 250 people grew within six years, and this has gone on to plant more churches. I doubt that approach would work this side of the Atlantic – Brits and Europeans are much more reserved compared to my experience of the friendly, voluble sharing of booths in American diners. Life together has to culturally fit and eat, pray, tell is ideally suited to creating British-style pockets of friendship which can then grow into outposts of the Jesus-shaped community. This is good news.

Identifiable Jesus-shaped communities

Part of my Mennonite learning is that their congregations are identifiable Jesus-shaped communities. They are far more than Sunday-worship gatherings with midweek Bible-study groups tacked on. While few congregants share households in any coordinated way (though some do), they are all committed to sharing resources à la Acts 2:42–47, often eating together on Sundays as well as communally each midweek. They are also openly identifiably engaged in service projects within the neighbourhood. Their lifestyle is committed to nurturing new disciples and overtly creating communities of the kingdom of Jesus. It seems a distinct contrast from the almost anonymous Christianity of many British congregations.

When I am asked to lead or speak at church-leader conferences about radical Anabaptist learning for church life, I often recommend a technical book called *Creating Communities of the Kingdom*.[13] The title says it all. It was written by two Mennonites, with well-received ministries rooted in the experience and mission of such local communities/congregations on four continents. The vital mark is to facilitate a group of believers to be more Spirit-led, living Jesus-shaped values, sharing his message openly and locally in ways that mark out the group as a daily community and not a Sunday-based congregation.

Over a generation ago, one UK Christian publisher brought out a series of books, each featuring ten churches which shared distinctive ministries (*Ten Praying Churches*, *Ten Serving Churches*, *Ten Worshipping Churches* and so on).[14] As part of my research for this book, I lent four titles from that series to various friends, asking them to analyse what was distinctive about the churches featured across the series. Their answers were all the same at heart: each one of those churches had identified a distinctive Jesus-shaped practice or ministry and had adopted it as their first priority. All had grown healthily in leadership and numbers, though not all the churches still existed as some had lost sight of their primary vision and purpose. But for us, the key conclusion was that the creation of a Jesus-shaped community with multilevels of relationship, servanthood at its heart and a primary focus on mission will produce fruit given time, energy and patience. Remember that Christian poster which said God wants spiritual fruits not religious nuts? Eat, pray, tell is about bearing spiritual fruit from Jesus-shaped communities.

During my doctoral studies, I had to undertake a research project about a particular nature or aspect of the church. Part of my problem was that I have never felt comfortable with the simple concept of church as the gathering of Christians on a Sunday, but that is how most of the academic research literature treated the church – much like defining a cow as a kind of animal that had a leg at each corner and mooed on certain occasions. Churches do not have to have a leg at each corner, be that a robed choir, a Sunday school or whatever, and they certainly are not restricted to mooing (or hymn-singing) only on a Sunday. Where is any of that in the Bible?

What is in the Bible is the creation of a radical alternative travelling community of folk adjusting themselves to the call, words, works and ways of God. In the Hebrew Bible, it is a people struggling to come together during wilderness wanderings to become the people of God, called Israel, despite some horrible history of rape, murder and genocide. In the New Testament, it is those people whose lives have been transformed by the words, works and ways of Jesus of Nazareth choosing to live in countercultural ways.

I undertook much research for my doctorate; you get the book with its everyday conclusions; and the church is offered the challenge of eat, pray, tell – rather than wistfully chewing the cud, with a leg at each corner and mooing when prompted. We – you and I – have the opportunity of helping others to experience the reign of God via eat, pray, tell, by developing a Jesus-shaped community that is different from others' expectations and past cultural norms.

A 52/7 agenda

We are enjoined to 'always be prepared to give an answer to everyone who asks you to give the reason for the hope that you have' (1 Peter 3:15, NIV). The clarity of this translation explains the reason which underpins the 'tell' part of this book's thesis. It is our 52/7 agenda.

It was Archbishop William Temple, in his still-powerful, two-volume commentary on John's Gospel, who began distinct advocacies about cross-cultural and mutually serving mission practices. One of his examples was Jesus asking the Samaritan woman for a drink of water (John 4:4–15); that is, Jesus asks her to do something for *him*. Jesus creates mutuality, across a racial divide which normally involved suspicion and hatred. We are striving to build Jesus' egalitarian new society.

While I am quite explicit that eat-pray-tell hosts must never charge nor ask for money from guests, we need to learn how to create mutuality. I have little problem with many of the regular, frequent eat-pray-tell groups where the host provides the main course but arranges with several guests on different occasions to bring side salads, dessert, bread or fruit juice. Part of the everyday agenda of the egalitarian gospel of Jesus is to create mutuality in serving one another.

Archbishop Temple helps us understand that mutual sharing blurs the boundaries between host and guest, facilitating the easier explanation of why we are doing what we do. Temple offers a complementary challenge to that of his later successor Williams in making us face the gospel's subversion of 'power' and 'powerlessness'. As 52/7 Christians, we need to understand both the practice and the theory, however tough.

Eat, pray, tell is not a lightweight commitment. We would be foolish to expect religious revival from hosting a single supper evening for the neighbours. Congregations may be able to say that they will use four or five annual festival gatherings to encourage us to bring friends and neighbours along. But if eat, pray, tell becomes rooted in our month-by-month home-based pattern of mission, it creates a 52/7 agenda. It will impact our family life or our shift pattern as well as our leisure choices. If we heed this Jesus-shaped model properly, we have to create a time-consuming discipline of accompanying prayer alongside our preparation and hosting of those regular meals. But the more I read about the first Christians or later renewal movements, I realise that while those Christians accepted the necessary patient ferment of their mission, they were 52/7 in their commitment to seeing the reign of God become known afresh through Jesus-shaped communities.

Group discussion questions

1 How much do we understand Jesus' message of the reign of God in the Gospels to be subversive?

2 How much and why do we think that congregations in our neighbourhood are not seen as 52/7 Jesus-shaped communities?

3 Which would be the most difficult obstacles in our lives to prayerfully consider beginning an eat-pray-tell group? What could this discussion group do to help alleviate or change that pressure?

Becoming Jesus-shaped people

11

Shake the dust off your feet

I was just a couple of months away from leaving one of my former pastorates, when I received a phone call from a woman at the smallest of my three churches. She was the 'new organiser' – she had only been doing the job for 12 years! – of their women's meeting. She wanted me to lead and speak at their 50th-anniversary meeting, on the afternoon before my removal van arrived. It was to be a celebration, and 'even husbands and male drivers' were going to be allowed to stay, followed by a sit-down tea. Somewhat reluctantly, I accepted their invitation and began prayerfully preparing for the occasion.

I knew that this group originally had nearly 80 members. But, like the proverbial ten green bottles, it had been whittled down to low numbers through death, divorce and house moves. I knew that, during my few years there, the group had gained no new members but I was surprised, if not shocked, to find out that over the 50 years they had only garnered about a dozen new attendees. Allegedly, the purpose of the group was to meet the spiritual needs of women in the neighbourhood – a neighbourhood in which there were many women without daytime work or family commitments. Sadly, this women's meeting was not living up to its own self-declared aim. But I encouraged their leaders to invite the whole church to come along, too – about another ten people – to share their sense of celebration.

The day came, and I preached as requested. I spoke about the laying down of burdens and Jesus' injunction to 'shake off the dust from your feet', which was not requested (Matthew 10:14). I had prepared well enough to carefully encourage them to recognise the difference between being an active-service unit and being a recruitment organisation, and to reflect individually upon what they were celebrating. We even had the birthday cake brought to the front, lit 50 candles on it and asked 'the committee' to gather around and blow them out. Many of the other members later engaged me in informal conversation about the changes they hoped to see.

I moved to a new ministry, but within a year that monthly women's meeting had changed – and my successor invited me back to see it. It is now a *weekly* lunch club for both women and men, serving soup and sandwiches prepared by the younger, *and some new*, members, followed by 'favourite hymns around the piano' for 20 minutes. By celebrating what has been, then recognising the need to prayerfully review a particular activity (or type of meeting) and identifying new needs, positive change can be wrought.

Sometimes we do not review our congregational life well enough to note that local needs have changed. To 'shake off the dust from our feet' can be creative.

When mission goes wrong

A friend of mine is a vicar in a garrison town, so he understands all too clearly the nature of an active-service unit. He frequently uses this as an analogy in his Sunday preaching and midweek Bible studies for a congregation that includes many military families. Because of the transient nature of military postings, his congregation is only too aware of the continual need to attract new folks into the life of the church, as they regularly see friends and neighbours move elsewhere. My friend knows if that congregation's mission goes awry, it will quickly die.

The mission of the church is God's – not ours. It is not simply about 'bums on seats' – though enough of those can help avoid difficult questions or visits from the archdeacon or area minister! – but about becoming more fully a Jesus-shaped community. This means not only creating a relevant worship and preaching life, which gathers people in praise, biblical reflection and prayer. We need also to create an accompaniment of welcoming activity, both for the newcomer and the mature believer, and of meeting the needs of ageing or infirm churchgoers and ostracised folk in our neighbourhood. Mission has a big agenda.

It is not God's mission which goes wrong – but our human desires and (in)ability to deliver what God is asking of us.

Mission goes wrong for two reasons:

- We fail to listen to God's call either directly or indirectly through the life and needs of the surrounding world or neighbourhood. Think how that women's meeting transformed itself into something which was more locally appropriate and brought growth in numbers.
- We get too immersed in both the business and busyness of maintaining the superstructure or artifice of the church. This can be in the detail of upholding a particular pattern of Sunday worship, practically maintaining an inappropriate suite of premises, or building too large a midweek programme for too few people to support or lead it, resulting in the breakdown or departure of key leaders. This prevents the creation of a prayerful strategic response to God's invitation to make all things new (Revelation 21:5).

The great practicality of eat, pray, tell is that it is a defining piece of mission strategy that is home-based, informal and able to be easily realigned by the addition of an extra (on-message, church-friendly) guest to help redefine its trajectory. Partly because eat, pray, tell echoes Jesus' narrative and is uncomplicated in what we need to do, it is relatively easy to make it a major part of our God-defined mission within our neighbourhood.

Deconstructing the church

The purpose of this book is *not* to assassinate the church. However, there is a growing body of well-researched literature, whether academic study, theological reflection or denominational statistical surveys, that demonstrates that the church in Britain is failing. Not just failing in its mission but dying on its feet, in many locations.

Unlike that previously mentioned garrison-town congregation, which would face a rapid demise if it lost its mission imperative, the death of other churches is often slow as members die or melt away. This is despite the fact there are many vibrant congregations and church leaders with integrity, exercising people-oriented ministry.

Such analysis has rightly given rise within the Christian world to a host of new literature and conferences which recognise this. With titles that include such phrases as 'Post-Christian', 'After Christendom', or 'Restoring Jesus' practice of…', these papers and seminars have much to commend them *if* they result in decisive change towards mission and new hope.

Whatever the merits and demerits of the UK having an established church, there are frequent, sometimes justified calls to recognise that the country is now multicultural and no longer simply Christian. Too many churchgoers in Britain are lulled into a false sense of security about the church's survival because:

- Remembrance Sunday, Christmas and Easter services are televised
- there are weekly BBC national radio broadcasts of Christian worship
- bishops sit in the House of Lords and daily prayers are said in the Commons
- there were religious assemblies when they went to school
- they believe that Parliament, under the leadership of prime ministers such as Margaret Thatcher (daughter of a Methodist

preacher) and Theresa May (a vicar's daughter and practising Anglican), will never allow the church's demise

- the church continues to survive despite a growing critique and cross-questioning by humanists, believers in scientism, comedians, media pundits and New Age thinkers
- someone else will keep it going
- they believe it will outlast their lifetime
- they know a church which has lots of worshippers – even if they do not go there!

All this is a sad indictment, and often by those who are the most vociferous critics of new patterns of mission.

In English towns and cities like Swindon, Wolverhampton or Sunderland, each with populations exceeding one-quarter of a million, where just a generation or so ago there were a dozen or more Methodist congregations, now there are only two or three. Most UK school children know more about Islam than they do about Methodism. Britain's faith perspectives are rapidly changing. When half-million-strong cities like Leeds do not have a single Christian bookshop, how do local Christians browse through faith-based books that might help their discipleship and mission?

When I was a volunteer retail chaplain, I sat through a somewhat embarrassing presentation by a commercial architect. He contrasted the frequent redesign of retail premises with the failure of churches to review the adequacy of their premises, that is, to ask what makes a building fit-for-purpose and welcoming. He also pointed out that normally it took oversized buildings, undersized finances, dry rot, road schemes or demographic changes to force congregations to undertake such a review. I suppose that I could not expect him to include God's missionary demands upon us.

Within the church, there are many jokes and too many snide asides about how few churchgoers are willing to accept change. But change is a necessary part of listening to God. Repentance and faith require personal change. A community's life in the Spirit brings renewal – change, by another name. If we fail to change as God invites, we share in the deconstruction of the church which that divine one called into being and continues to call into new beginnings.

The late Walter Wink, a biblical theologian, spoke of this in his excellent *Unmasking the Powers*. In it he tells the story of one of his former students, Melinda, a hard-working pastor who finds her ministry and 'God's call to change' continually rebuffed because strong individuals keep undermining the congregational leadership with their sniping and outright opposition to proposed changes. Wink notes, 'there is a deeper, more sinister, though unconscious reason these people want to keep their church, and to keep it precisely as they have it, in a condition of perpetual morbidity. [Their] low self-esteem… is transferred to the church.' God does not enable change *if* the people are unwilling to accept the personal changes and challenge required.

Wink comments: 'God calls us to transform the church, and yet only God can bring that change about.'[15] The church's only God-given right to exist is precisely because of its faithfulness to the Creator's missionary call, Jesus-shaped discipleship and Spirit-driven communities of faith. We return to this creative agenda in the next chapter.

If humanity attempts to remake the church in its own image rather than in God's image, revealed by the words and ways of Jesus, it will deconstruct what God wants for the church. No wonder many congregations atrophy and die – simply because of their own self-centredness. Virtually every Christian in Britain knows of a church which has withered and died. But have we the courage and realism to explore why?

Congregational realism and denominational strategy

By denominational strategy, I do not mean just identifiable denominations, such as the Methodist Church or the United Reformed Church, nor parochially based state churches, such as the Church of England or the Church of Scotland, nor simply those conferences of like-minded churches, such as the UK's Baptist Union, the Congregational Federation or North American Mennonite groupings. I also include such groupings of churches as those from the pioneer and other new church networks.

I have had the rich privilege of working ecumenically in many locations and different contexts, and what has become evident throughout my ministry is the decreasing number attending many churches and the increasing burden (both in time and finances) of maintaining clergy – church leadership – and buildings. Something has to give. I have Anglican acquaintances struggling in united benefices of more than six congregations, each with their own buildings, as well as Methodist and URC friends looking after multiple churches in different communities that have no significant link or interest in the other places. The increasing numbers of clergy with burnout or taking early retirement counts that cost. It's time for a change.

Denominations are having to think radically, challenging congregations to work together and use more home-based strategies, such as eat, pray, tell, to greater effect. By all means retain a single, much-used worship centre, which can also host Alpha courses, Messy Church and specifically Christian activities, in each centre of population, possibly paying its way through playgroup and other community usage, hosting pensioners' lunches and so forth. But it is time for change. In their stimulating book *The Church Comes Home*, Robert and Julia Banks state, 'As home churches begin within denominational churches, more denominational facilitators with the vision and ability to encourage them will be required.'[16] In turn, this will enable the role of the clergy to seismically shift. It becomes easier to see how bi-vocational and non-stipendiary educators, facilitators and church leaders will need to be recognised in each geographical community. Perhaps only the area ministers and bishops, providing oversight, should be full-time and stipendiary in most areas, something I have witnessed in Sweden and the Netherlands.

Elsewhere, from North American Mennonites and mainland European Anabaptists, I have become convinced of the practice of 'no meeting without eating'. If our more traditionalist Sunday congregations learned to experience more meals together, whether after Sunday worship or within their midweek home groups, it would make it much easier for Alpha course converts, Messy Church participants and eat-pray-tell guests to blend together with longer-believing folks as single Christian communities in each geographical neighbourhood.

When prayer, neighbourhood service (think food banks) and eating together (think Lent lunches, etc.) become the drivers for ecumenical sharing, the stupidity of not sharing buildings as well becomes apparent. In addition, why would we each all need our particular brand of church leader, when one person can facilitate our fuller sharing, mission and worship? Eat, pray, tell can be another good way for networking pastors to share both their burdens and new opportunities for mission, as previous chapters have indicated.

During my lifetime, I have seen the transformation of new church networks. During my sixth-form grammar school days, some classmates joined 'house churches' because they met in someone's front room. The growth of those groups led to them renting halls and church spaces for Sunday worship. Commentators then called them 'new churches', because they had outgrown the concept of being a house church. Many went on to refurbish commercial premises and redundant church buildings to establish stronger neighbourhood ministries, while establishing networks of congregations. Yet some are now struggling with the same challenges as more historic denominations. Still fewer of them have even considered the 'no meeting without eating' mantra.

Many mission-oriented readers will already be familiar with the concepts of 'fresh expressions', 'cross currents' and 'emerging churches' to describe the next swathe of mission cells and communities. Unlike the previous generation's new church movement, these latest initiatives utilise food- and meal-sharing far more effectively *and often* in their outreach to friends, neighbours and contacts. I receive far more invitations from these newest ecclesial initiatives and historic denominations to speak (and advocate) eat, pray, tell than from the new church movement congregations. As Stuart Murray, an experienced church planter, has written in *Changing Mission*, 'the significance of emerging church is not numerical… Emerging church has provocative similarities to previous renewal movements…'[17]

Perhaps a renewed congregational realism is creeping in, whether that is from a family-based fresh expression or a shrinking congregation in an outmoded, now poorly located building. With some safeguards, every Christian group can plan to use eat, pray, tell as part of its mission strategy. I was really pleased and encouraged that the URC's Yorkshire Synod (their equivalent of a diocese) sent a copy of my *Hospitality and Community after Christendom* to each of its local churches, to encourage their meal-sharing and enrich their hospitality. Pleased? Yes, because this shows a significant denominational strategy, which is now bearing fruit. Perhaps this also needs to happen, and much more widely, with *Eat, Pray, Tell*. If your pastor did not recommend this book to you, why not buy him or her a copy?

In the next chapter we can look at the creative agenda of how this is beginning to occur. But if we are serious about utilising eat, pray, tell, we need to be assured that we have the appropriate checks, balance and practice to include it in our mission strategy.

Good eat-pray-tell practice

Denominations and other networks are not a bad thing, as they can help us. In today's world, we need to be very much aware of safeguarding issues, and our wider church authorities have specialist advisers who can help us in that.

Here are seven simple guidelines that any responsible congregational strategy would advocate:

- Clearly, no one wants to stop a solo pensioner inviting a similar near neighbour in for tea, coffee or supper. But be aware of who you are inviting into your home.
- Generally, always host small groups in pairs, whether you are a couple or not. Do not lay yourself open to accusation. If you live alone, why not ask one of the same-gender elders of your church to be your co-host (*but let them read this book first*).
- Invite only those who are obviously over 18 and who could not be classed as vulnerable adults, graciously accepting others' boundaries as important; for example, plan for good conversation but also to enable folks to leave as they need to for babysitters, buses or whatever.
- Begin by only inviting near-neighbours whom you know. This is more difficult in rural areas, so find another way to know who the person is before inviting them. Do you meet them regularly in the shop or the village pub? Or do you have a mutual acquaintance who has talked about them?
- If you decide to invite families, have several co-hosts and insist that parents remain with their children, with parents undertaking 'toileting'/first aid for their own brood. Preferably use a community hall for such all-age gatherings in the winter, or an open space for barbecues in the summer. Think before inviting!
- Avoid serving alcohol. People have different tolerance levels to alcohol and may have to drive afterwards. A can of beer at a summer barbecue or a glass of wine at a wine-and-cheese evening is probably okay, but you are hosting a get-to-know-you meal not

a booze-up. Good mineral water, natural cordials and fruit juices can provide wise, refreshing alternatives.

- Never ask for money or a contribution towards costs. If a co-host or regular guest brings the dessert, or your church underwrites your costs, that is okay.

Shaking the dust off our feet also has the meaning of rousing ourselves to a fresh challenge. Eat, pray, tell is such an opportunity.

Group discussion questions

1 Which piece of our congregation or ecumenical group agenda should we consider 'shaking off the dust from our feet'?

2 How easy would it be to adopt an eat-pray-tell strategy within our own neighbourhood?

3 What are the key obstacles in local Christian thinking which mean that we do not easily engage with new patterns of mission activity?

4 Can you identify together any other local guidelines which you should observe in developing an eat-pray-tell strategy?

12

Principles for a missionary community

As a child I learned to play the recorder. This helped me to learn some musical principles, which in turn helped me to begin playing the guitar as a teenager and the flute as an adult. The practice of doing some simple coordinated actions meant others could recognise what I was playing – amazingly! They too could learn the tune.

The same is true for the church. We have to begin simply, then practice, develop and offer what others can comfortably recognise and enjoy. As they share within that, they begin to learn the Jesus-community's underlying principles, which are rooted in his words, works and ways. They can then learn the tune, with all the melody and harmony, which Jesus enables us to know in sharing his life with all its fullness.

By now, I trust that you can accept that eat, pray, tell is a practice of the church, biblically, historically and contemporarily, which reveals Jesus' new kind of life together. In simply living out that eat-pray-tell discipleship lifestyle, we are celebrating and reaffirming some central principles of Jesus' outward-looking community. In this chapter, we can see this more clearly.

Reconstructing the Jesus-shaped community

The purpose of this book is to affirm the task of rebuilding the Jesus-shaped community in every neighbourhood, through the grace and help of God's renewing Spirit.

I am often called to speak about the Jesus-shaped community, its theology, mission and practices. As my teaching, conference-speaking and Sunday preaching ministry continue to evolve, I am noting how often I quote key well-tested phrases from others either as part of my presentations or in answer to public questions. These seem to resonate with what God is repeatedly saying and my hearers acknowledge that. Let me offer you just some of these.

'In the Gospels, meal sharing is a test of social reconstruction,' writes Ched Myers, a peace organiser and Quaker activist, in his commentary on Mark's Gospel, *Binding the Strong Man*. John Dominic Crossan, the New Testament scholar, wrote, 'at the heart of the original Jesus movement, a shared egalitarianism of spiritual and material resources developed'. Christine Pohl recognises how much that affects our lives and priorities too: 'To offer significant hospitality from our homes will require some re-thinking of the relationship between work and home, the living relationships we choose, and the significance we assign to our time away from work.' John Howard Yoder, the Mennonite theologian, repeatedly points out that, 'What the New Testament is talking about wherever the theme is "breaking of bread" is that people were actually sharing with one another their ordinary day-to-day material sustenance… Bread eaten together is economic sharing.'[18]

For our purposes, you will have noticed two things in these quoted remarks. First, how much meal-sharing is part of the significant everyday practice of the vibrant Jesus community. Second, that this is being said by respected, widespread, ecumenical voices within our own generation. In practising eat, pray, tell, we imitate the pattern of the earthly Jesus community and can recognise the significance of 'sharing our bread' just as others already have done.

In the first centuries of that Jesus movement, within the era historians refer to as that of the church fathers, there is documentary evidence that Christians, through their practices of hospitality, shared meals, economic sharing and service to others, attracted the positive attention and interest of the surrounding pagan communities.

Alan Kreider, a Mennonite educator and church historian, wrote in his excellent book *The Patient Ferment of the Early Church* that by the fourth century, 'the Church had moved from being a meal society to being a worship assembly and their primary meeting had moved from dinner to breakfast. Another change had to do with the food that was served in the liturgies. The full meals that had characterised early Christian services were being replaced by symbolic tokens of bread and wine in a cultic meal.'[19] Kreider, along with other church and architectural historians, notes that as this seismic shift was occurring, the Christian congregations were shifting away from a home-based culture into specialist buildings, basilicas and temples. Jesus' way of advocating mission in user-friendly, home-based contexts was unsubtly lost. Eat, pray, tell is a dynamic statement to return to that community-building, user-friendly, home-based practicality.

Mission was – and is – an organic practice of both living simply and simply living as Jesus asked, by sharing one's daily bread and concern for others in service to them that they too come to believe in the saving grace and reign of God, revealed in Jesus.

I had the amazing privilege of learning afresh much of this life-affirming theology and practice from my former spiritual director Lesslie Newbigin, who was a missionary bishop in India before becoming a world-renowned missiologist. He repeatedly privately and publicly advocated that Jesus 'created and left a community' that celebrated the reign of God in every aspect of life individually and collectively. My friend Noel Moules, a respected Anabaptist educator, speaks of Jesus' legacy as 'a community with a meal'. Both eat, pray, tell and a home-based mission strategy are essential if we are to build a robust Jesus-shaped community. Paul, the archetypal church planter, relied on others' homes to help build up the New Testament communities.

Kreider's thesis is correct: we can only build up the body of Christ, as Jesus-shaped communities, by the patient ferment of the church itself. But it is the very patience and ferment of conversation within our eat-pray-tell strategy that makes it successful as our guests are gradually drawn into recognising that every shared meal celebrates the reign of God.

It seems that many Christians today are having to find home-based strategies as the nature of our corporate Christian lives changes. In several parts of Britain, I know of small networks of radical Christians who gather in each other's homes to share a peace-meal.[20] When London's Wood Green Mennonite Church regrettably had to disband, they continued to meet, albeit less frequently, to share their prayers and stories over occasional meals. In the West Country, a small quasi-Orthodox network of Trinitarian Christians meet regularly for prayer or to say mass in various garden oratories, then have a bring-and-share meal. The members of a Pennine village chapel that had to close because of subsidence continue to meet in a few larger homes and have adopted the 'no meeting without eating' mantra. With each of these groups, I am in close contact with some of their people to encourage them into an eat-pray-tell strategy for growth.

Since its publication in 1998, I have given several copies of the revised edition of *The Church Comes Home* to leaders of under-pressure groups such as those mentioned in the previous paragraph. That book encourages the growth of what we now often term 'fresh expressions': a small town-wide network of home-based Christian groups who use shared meals and prayer on every occasion of gathering.[21] Now as denominations need to review building needs, consolidating some, closing others, a fellowship that is rooted in a home-based network of committed Christian groups is not to be feared but nurtured. In doing this, it is only a short step to the adoption of eat, pray, tell as a primary mode of mission.

A bring-and-share meal, or pot-luck dinner as North Americans call them, can lift the burden from a solo cook when large groups are gathering. But eat, pray, tell thrives on its smaller, relational style, so is less of a catering demand. How many folks can fit around your table – if you have one? Or just plan a fork supper (no knives needed) if people are sitting around your lounge on various chairs.

Eat, pray, tell is an adaptable strategy for cooks and caterers just as much as it is for every kind of church or congregation. We make it fit our circumstances, creativity, conversation and culinary skill – wherever we are. Community is created because we make ourselves vulnerable and blur the lines between host and guest.

Growing the church

I do not believe 'the church' is a dead concept in our post-Christendom, multicultural and increasingly post-Christian Britain. The very fact that fewer people have grown up in the life of the church, or receive quality religious education during their schooldays, presents God's people with exciting new opportunities.

In the history of the church right through to my childhood, people lived in a television-less Britain, often in colder, more cramped and draughtier homes with less comfortable furniture than is true today. Then, 'going to church' engaged you with other people and provided the opportunity to hear both exposition and interpretation of why the world is as it is and to escape from the four walls of an at times bleak existence; it thus proved attractive. In twenty-first century Britain, however, technology, comfort and the availability of information are all home-based. This is also why local pubs are closing faster than churches in many neighbourhoods. Socialisation and communication are increasingly found in the home.

This is why eat, pray, tell is an appropriate strategy, and *one* of the primary ones, for the church in today's generation. But there are few circumstances where it should be the sole strategy for growing the church. For reasons of accountability and integrity, eat, pray, tell should be plugged into the life of a local congregation or an ecumenically agreed fresh expression. It is a huge ask for a local eat-pray-tell host couple to provide the ongoing, broader nurture of those whose lives increasingly celebrate the reign of God in following after the words, works and ways of Jesus.

We need to recognise the patterns of the post-Gospel New Testament communities to move the agenda onward. Clearly Acts 2:42–47 provides us with a key pattern, if not a blueprint for action. But in anything beyond a cursory examination of the New Testament letters, we can recognise communication to a city- or region-wide network of home-based congregations in the letters to the Corinthians, Thessalonians, Galatians, Romans and so on. Even the pastoral epistles and task-driven Pauline letters, such as Philemon, recognise a number of local leaders who have groups of Christians meeting in their homes. In the interim, between Acts 2 and all these letters, we can recognise the importance and vitality of the home-based community-creating initiatives that planted churches in places like Philippi, Jerusalem and Joppa. We should also remember that such groups had their primary gatherings in the evenings with a main meal, only later having purpose-built meeting houses and sharing only token refreshment (as they moved their main gathering to Sunday morning). Eat, pray, tell is both a Jesus initiative and a New Testament principle.

Hebrew faith was an event-centred journey; think Passover, Pentecost, Rosh Hashanah, Shavuot and Sukkoth, among others, providing an annual cycle of celebration, sharing food and extended gathering. Christians need to learn from this. Local congregations who utilise Christian celebrations or festivals can create their own cycle of extended gatherings, when sharing food will make participants of neighbourhood eat-pray-tell groups feel welcome into the wider church. Let me offer some examples:

- a Saturday-evening harvest supper, with dessert and songs of thanksgiving sung at the tables;

- a well-organised, non-preachy festival of lessons and carols, followed by mulled wine, cheese and crackers, then mince pies;
- a Shrove Tuesday pancake early evening event, with races for the children, savoury and sweet pancakes plus the launch of a local Lenten challenge;
- an Easter morning breakfast (after a short sunrise service?) with both boiled and mini-chocolate eggs and hot rolls;
- a Pentecost party, with biodegradable, releasable helium balloons, bring-and-share food and bright clothing.

Such a cycle would allow eat-pray-tell hosts to invite any or all of their guests at any of these annual moments, always 'only a few weeks away', appropriately to experience the life of the wider church. You do not grow a healthy plant by overwatering or overmulching it; you give it enough nurture and then time-appropriate moment to flourish, long before you put it in the bigger plot for onward growth. Hosts need to exercise such similar discernment, introducing their eat-pray-tell guests into the wider church. There is also continuity in 'no meeting without eating'.

Wise leaders and sensible hosts recognise that growing the church is a patient ferment in which we make haste slowly. It might be that after attending a couple of these types of annual events, our guests are ready to consider joining an Alpha (or similar congregational-based) course or bringing their children to our Messy Church activities and so on – again, with 'no meeting without eating' helping to build both a bridge and continuity into the wider church.

Developing a prayer-laden strategy for mission

The whole eat-pray-tell pattern of mission needs to be undergirded by prayer. This is equally true whether it is being adopted as a congregational programme or it is the initiative of a single (potentially more isolated) Christian household. But, as my friend Allan Armstrong ODP has written, such 'prayer requires clarity of intention and commitment to its development'.[22] Neither eat, pray, tell nor prayer can be this year's fad or focus for a congregation. Jesus-shaped mission is rooted in the soil of fertile prayer.

I do not intend to repeat what I have already said in Part 2, except to underline my affirmation that committed prayer must be a vital part of every Christian's discipleship. This is true whether or not they are engaged in eat, pray, tell.

As with any strategy for mission, eat, pray, tell must have the ground prepared by seeding it with prayer. I am an ongoing supporter of the Mission England practice of prayer triplets – groups of three individuals who gather regularly, preferably weekly, to pray for just three of each other's concerns. Those individuals commit to praying daily for the six concerns raised by their companions, between their meetings, as well as their own three nominated needs. The key factor here is that a discipline of intercessory prayer is being fostered as each of the participants takes on responsibility for bearing each particular concern before God daily. Such intercession develops real power and integrity of prayer, whether the nominated concerns are for an individual, an eat-pray-tell gathering or a global issue.

Whether in a widespread rural parish or a busy urban environment, such prayer triplets can be an ideal way of nurturing the prayer life of a congregation, whether large or small. Equally, it can be an ideal way for three different eat-pray-tell hosts to pray for their home-based gatherings, their guests and their guests' concerns in due course. But remember that gossip about others' business is unbiblical and contrary to Jesus' words and ways, so such prayer triplets need to focus on the prayer issues.

In several geographically varied locations, I have utilised Bill Hybels' *Too Busy Not to Pray* book and study programme creatively to help revitalise the prayer life of busy individuals within congregations, where it seemed too much was already happening without enough supportive prayer.[23]

My task here is to encourage you to have a clear commitment to a prayer strategy. It is *not* to pull you away from your congregation's own practice *nor* to undermine the teaching of your pastor and elders. Deepening our prayer life is a matter of lifelong discipline and ferment. But, pray we must *if* we are to follow Jesus' words and ways.

Being committed afresh to prayer will change our lives too. As Søren Kierkegaard, the Danish philosopher and religious thinker, succinctly wrote: 'The function of prayer is not to influence God, but to change the nature of the one who prays.'[24] We may well be the ones with the answer to others' prayers in the way we share our resources and use our time (see page 103).

Recognising our missionary principles

Jesus said, 'I have come that they may have life – life in all its fullness' (John 10:10, author's translation). Some of our guests with busy family lives or dependent ageing relatives or who live alone should discover that eating a well-cooked meal, prepared by others, with healthy conversation is a source of blessing, a different kind of community and a sign of 'life in all it fullness'. In our growing acquaintance, even nascent friendship, eat, pray, tell is a declaration of desire to bring Jesus' life of fullness to others.

The great commission from Matthew 28, which we explored at the start of Part 3, is about discipling. It is about enabling others to follow after the words, works and ways of Jesus. Making disciples is a missionary principle.

Jesus was challenged by the religious leaders of his day about the greatest commandments. His answer was twofold. The first part was to love God with everything we have – this becomes evident in our commitment and priority to God in prayer and service. The other part was to love our neighbours as ourselves, which is exactly what eat, pray, tell enables for us. I know of such hosts who have had non-believing neighbours knock on the door to ask if they could come too.

Many missionaries in the UK and elsewhere will say it is how we live in our neighbourhoods that will declare our missionary principles and practice. Only when others see that will they listen to our words or those of Jesus. Eat, pray, tell is a patient ferment of witness and sharing with our neighbours. I humbly commend it to you as a Jesus-shaped pattern that will bring others to acknowledge his reign and share in his life with all its fullness.

Group discussion questions

1 How well are we convinced that the 'no meeting without eating' mantra is both vital to the mission of the church and a Jesus-shaped strategy for bringing others to share in the reign of God?

2 In 'growing the church' what other kind of events can you envisage nurturing to help folks' inward journey towards a fuller sharing in the life of the church?

3 What examples can we share from our own congregational life when we have become the answer to the prayers of identified intercession?

4 Which other core Jesus-defined principles would you need to add to begin an eat-pray-tell strategy of mission?

13

Eat, pray, tell:
the shape of things to come?

By now, I hope you can accept my belief that shared meals are a central part of the church, biblically, historically and contemporarily. After I had led a Greenbelt seminar about this, one member of the audience was applauded after she asked, 'Are you saying that shared meals are the life and soul of the Jesus party?' Her question invites further comment here, as well as the answer I gave to her and the appreciative Greenbelt audience.

The New Testament, in its description of both Jesus' earthly ministry and that of the first-century church, has meals as a central and essential part of its sharing of life. Theologically, we can say such sharing is a central and essential part of the corporate celebration of God's provision. This and the recognition of God's grace in salvation are at the core of Jesus' manifesto and God's *shalom*. How perceptive was my questioner actually being when asking about this as the 'life and soul of the Jesus party'? Her question certainly has stuck in my mind over the years. Some Christians liken the corporate Christian life to that of an ongoing party – prefiguring that of the heavenly banquet – because it continually celebrates the salvation and provision of the God whom we know in Jesus. I write this final chapter during the 2017 UK general election campaign, and I know that 'the Jesus party' is not a partisan self-interest group as the present posturing of our several political parties so clearly reveal about themselves.

But it is my contention that from the days of New Testament following after Jesus, through the life of the early church and later countercultural, radical Christian movements, to the present day, the sharing of meals as a precursor to shared discipleship has been vital. How often today do denominational confirmation classes use sausage sizzles, McDonald's evenings and shared meals as a way of securing commitment to those courses? This chapter addresses the question of why and how it should, once again, be a decisive part of the Christian community's growth, grace, generosity and its future.

What have we learned?

Biblically we need to be clear that:

- Jesus' own public, earthly ministry is packed with the sharing of not just meals but of food itself. We can parse the Gospels to show that Jesus' ministry was roughly one-quarter such sharing of food and meals. (The other three quarters are: prayer/spiritual wrestling; preaching and teaching; healing.)
- Whether Jesus is sending out the twelve (Matthew 10:1–7; Mark 6:7–13) or the 72 (Luke 10:1–12), the pattern is similar – the disciples go out in pairs, adopting a bespoke strategy of eat, pray, tell.
- The life of the immediate post-Pentecost community of believers shared quite distinctively in daily meals (Acts 2:42–47). This was in such massive contrast to the common practice of their Roman oppressors' gluttonous feasts and the Jewish cultic meals or festivals that Luke noted it in Acts.
- Paul's missionary journeys rely on a local family, couple or business person welcoming him and his co-leaders into their home to first begin, then later to carry on, their mission and church-planting. During such hospitality, Paul built strong, candid relationships with those who were to lead the church in that area; naturally, that must have occurred over significant time and the sharing of meals. A specific example is Paul's relationship with Philemon, to whom Paul can address a single-issue letter strongly advocating that Philemon accepts back the runaway slave Onesimus, 'as a

Christian brother', rather than facially branding or executing the miscreant servant.

- Likewise, the letters of John show a similar pattern of relationships with that itinerant apostle. How could such mentor–church leader relationships have been built without the spending of time together and shared hospitality? Biblical scholars such as Oscar Cullman and Raymond Brown have written about the web of interwoven leadership relationships, rooted in mutual sharing.[25]

What is important to recognise is that these itinerant bearers of the good news, and even their letters, would have travelled slowly – whether on foot or by sea – necessitating time and meals in each locality. It would take a much longer book than this to analyse each Gospel, each New Testament letter and Revelation to cover each written example, but this broad-brush survey makes us aware of each circumstance's eat-pray-tell reality.

Historically, we have already recognised some examples from Celtic churches, monastic settlements and radical church history.

- In the previous chapter, I quoted Alan Kreider, who used primary sources to show how the Christendom church moved from being a community that shared an evening main meal to being a Sunday morning congregation sharing a token Eucharist while abandoning the practice of eating together or mainly giving food to the poor.
- In the early days of Anabaptism, during the 16th-century Radical Reformation, their itinerant leaders relied on the hospitality of supporters and patterns of eat, pray, tell to share the radical nature of following after Jesus.
- During the Tudor and subsequent persecutions of English Roman Catholics, fugitive priests travelled between the estates of their wealthy supporters, ministering to those families as well as the villagers. Eat, pray, tell was a natural strategy for them, too.
- Various 17th-century English county or Assize records demonstrate that George Fox and the first Quakers were often convicted for

their subversive patterns of association, brought about by their understanding of eat, pray, tell.

- Every British denomination which had its own overseas missionary society, such as the Baptist Missionary Society, have 19th- and 20th-century published documentation of their own use of Jesus' eat-pray-tell strategy – even if they normally do not name it as such.

More personally:

- During the ongoing growth of the UK's 19th-century Restorationist movement, my great-grandfather was an itinerant evangelist within the Churches of Christ. He planted many churches, returning almost annually to 'encourage or admonish' those congregations and help train further leaders. To achieve this, he had to leave his family behind for weeks (and often months) on their Surrey smallholding with its many rural privations (no electricity, only well water and earth closets). But in the manner of the disciples, New Testament apostles and later radical church leaders, he would stay with a local church family, eating shared meals and sometimes sleeping in the unheated outhouse. But to gather new congregations together, he would encourage a few converts to meet daily together for prayer, Bible study and simple meals. After some weeks, he would leave them to draw in more neighbours, via an eat-pray-tell strategy and return a year later for a week-long tent mission. He would always return for the opening service of whatever building that embryonic congregation adopted, famously splitting the panels of a brand-new pulpit as he thumped out Jesus' demands, staying again for some days – enjoying the hospitality of the local church leaders.

- One of my great privileges as a Christian, a writer and a community theologian is to spend time learning together with different local congregations around Britain. Often we will be involved with a Saturday conference, including a shared lunch, as well as Sunday worship. Sometimes there will also be a Friday or Saturday evening table talk, when a group of 10–20 local leaders and their partners gather for a meal and discussion. Janice (my partner) and I will often stay with one of the church leaders. When our weekend topic is hospitality, eat, pray, tell or something similar, the shared meals and life together underpin the teaching and learning. It also begins new and furthers existing friendships.

Eat, pray, tell takes many forms, but its key aim is to build strong human relationships. Yet we can find its outworking in several current church practices. This chapter seeks to affirm the breadth of such ministries, so for each topic I offer a few examples known to me.

Eat, pray, tell

This book found its genesis in three things. First, simply the experience of different folks running their own varied expressions of eat, pray, tell. Second, my own academic study of how churches utilise shared meals in mission, then talking about this in sermons, seminars and conferences. Third, the increasing requests from individuals about the hows and whys, and also from church leaders who want to know its theological and biblical provenance. So here we are.

As the years progress, my database of how others have adopted eat, pray, tell is growing:

- A couple of my acquaintance (former church members) relocated to the Chilterns and joined the only local church – an Anglican one. They were pleased it ran Alpha well but were disappointed that there was no real congregational tradition of shared meals, except for the annual harvest supper. Several villagers came to Alpha but could not make the transition into the Sunday congregation because they missed the intimacy of its shared meal. So, with the blessing of their vicar and the parish's Alpha team, they invited those who had stayed somewhat in touch with the church, whether through carol services or coffee mornings, to join their eat-pray-tell fortnightly meal.

- While working with Mennonites in north London, I got to know a couple who retired to the Cheviot hills, where they began attending the local Methodist Church. When it became too expensive to maintain the building, that chapel closed and rather than drive eight miles to worship each Sunday, they began a fortnightly eat-pray-tell group in their home, initially attracting former local churchgoers from their own hamlet. I believe they are church, even though they don't moo or have four legs, as their former chapel congregation *may* have tried to do!

- In metropolitan West Yorkshire, one postgraduate couple, frustrated by the insularity of their local United Reformed Church, opened the large basement kitchen of their back-to-back house on a monthly Saturday lunchtime for a hot buffet, with chat based around that day's newspapers. It's not quite café church, but it is an open-house eat, pray, tell. To be fair, as the elders of that URC have heard about this initiative, some have attended and are giving support to the couple in this ministry, rather than pressuring them to do something else.

- In Glasgow, one Church of Scotland couple began an eat-pray-tell group, simply by inviting everyone from their tenement stairwell for a monthly supper and conversation.

- When I lived in France, we had a 'closed' eat-pray-tell group but others heard about it, either through the ecumenical Sunday congregation or the monthly home groups, and the initiative has spread to more households, opening up eat-pray-tell groups to predominantly English and Dutch ex-pats.

- In a rundown part of Deeside, a Roman Catholic couple, inspired by Dorothy Day and the Catholic Worker movement, heard me speak at a conference about eat, pray, tell. They have since emailed to say they now have a group of predominantly single (and 'often broken') folk, for whom their group has become 'a journey into community'. Hallelujah!

Increasingly, I am being asked to speak at seminars about eat, pray, tell. Whether in local congregations, multi-parishes, Methodist circuits or at regional conferences, I seem to be pushing at an open door in advocating this grass-roots initiative as part of Christian outreach. The subsequent response and questions I receive on the Internet likewise reveals the level of interest as well as the excitement and encouragement of people across Britain and beyond who are just getting on and starting eat-pray-tell gatherings at an appropriate level. There is no nationally defined nor coherent eat-pray-tell strategy, except in the hosts' response to the Spirit's prompting. That may seem messy, but for me eat, pray, tell can be church: is there really anything that is proto-church? Messy Church is something else.

Messy Church

One of the gifts to the church in this millennium is the Messy Church initiative, which in the last decade has taken a strong grip on church life as well as mission thinking. The first Messy Church programme began in 2004 in an Anglican parish near Portsmouth. Since then, with all credit to the Bible Reading Fellowship, the movement has grown and developed, with both published literature and a network of local encouragers.[26]

There are five values or (principles) to Messy Church:

- Christ-centred – too many people dismiss Messy Church as a craft club, which it is not. It is a church in its own right. It may not have four legs and moo, as some traditionalists want of an identikit church, but this is a gathering of God's people, seeking to share the good news of Jesus.
- All-age – it is for adults and children to enjoy together. Not all adults understand that we are but children in the sight of our God, whom some address as Father. This is an expression of church, which is dynamic and heterogeneous.
- Creativity – the whole aim of Messy Church is that together young and old use hands-on activities to retell the stories of Jesus. Whether it is building an Easter garden, making banners, painting

posters or whatever form of craft, we declare that we are made in the image of the creator God.

- Hospitality – that same creator God is one who loves us so unconditionally that he sent his only begotten son (John 3:16) – but this is just the crown of God's creative provision to us. The nature of our hospitality at Messy Church is equally unconditional, whether it includes doughnuts, sandwiches, barbecued food or pie 'n' mash.

- Celebration – our God's unconditional love and provision tells the world that God wants us to have a 'life in all its fullness' (John 10:10), and we are encouraged to celebrate that. Newcomers to a church are far more likely to return and be encouraged by a real sense of joy and praise, whether musically or in the character of the leaders, as well the general cheeriness (but not a false bonhomie) in where and how we meet.

In researching and writing this book, I took time to visit and enjoy different experiences of Messy Church. I also contacted various church leaders online – many of whom willingly gave time or made Skype calls, sent photos and video clips, as well as e-assessments of their Messy Church journeys. Let me offer some examples:

- In the south Cotswolds, there is a Congregational chapel where the whole congregation participates in Messy Church on one Sunday each month, eating a bring-and-share lunch together at the end of their morning. They have witnessed a quiet influx of new families.

- Because the primary schools in their area close at Friday lunchtime, a small independent church in the Lancashire Pennines runs a Friday-afternoon Messy Church session during term time. In the winter, they serve pie 'n' mash but revert to barbecues during the blustery summer. This has become so popular with both adults and children that they have abandoned traditionalist Sunday school in favour of Messy Church on Fridays.

- In the so-called Bible belt of the M25 (the motorway that orbits London), there is a large Anglican church whose building dominates the high street. Fortnightly on Saturday mornings it hosts a well-funded Messy Church, which is attracting shoppers of all ages. Their vicar, with a neat line in slogan-bearing posters, advertises Messy Church with 'the family that prays together stays together', to gently convey the rule that the families who attend must do so together, so that Messy Church does not become a child-minding exercise. (But I do worry what his adverts appear to say to those who are part of broken or re-blended families.)

- In the Cardiff Bay area, one Welsh independent chapel had only 20 or so remaining members, who knew they might only have the chance for one last mission initiative. They chose a fortnightly midweek Messy Church activity, with alternating hotpots, Welsh stew and pasta meals served to all attendees. Their church has grown as five families came to faith and into the congregation. Messy Church continues for them.

- In an East Midlands city, Messy Church has grasped the vision of so many in a local Baptist congregation that it has requested anonymity while it excitedly redefines its future trajectory, mission and ministry.

Messy Church is becoming established as a key resource in the life of the church in the UK. Nearly three generations ago, H.A. Hamilton wrote a book called *The Family Church*, which changed patterns of both Sunday school and often parish worship. With good discernment, Hamilton foresaw that post-war Britain would need a new family-integrated pattern of Christian nurture.[27] His work led many to introduce children's addresses into congregational worship; these were often patronising but have evolved into what is often termed the 'family spot' and led to the introduction of more frequent all-age worship, particularly among free churches.

In discovering more about Messy Church, I believe it will become even more influential than Hamilton's theorising was. What I have witnessed is eat-pray-tell-with-a-creative-twist. People, children and adults, join in without any prerequisite faith demands – they always share food, learn how to pray and creatively explore the 'Jesus narrative' and their hosts' understandings of God's provision. It is too early to say, but Messy Church has the potential to be as important for mission as Alpha has been.

Alpha

I have already offered some reflections on Alpha and why it has such appeal. It has become an 'integrity franchise'. That is, churches offering Alpha effectively agree to run the programme in the manner prescribed: a meal-talk-discussion format, using the talks in their set order, and so forth. It is a matter of integrity to use the Alpha format and utilise Alpha resources, if a congregation is offering a course which they call Alpha. Alpha's own regional conferences prayerfully help churches adopt the package and format, backed up by county advisers as well as wide-ranging tried-and-tested published resources. In my opinion, Alpha has become a useful fast-track eat-tell-pray (yes, that order) gift to local churches that are within reach of literate seekers who can commit to its weekly schedule of journeying towards commitment.

A few years ago, Alpha publicised that over one million people had participated in an Alpha course. A friend of mine who is an Anglican vicar in professional south London assures me that there are always enough newcomers to the capital, and to his neighbourhood and parish, that Alpha has a lot more people to reach – so they will never run out of Alpha guests. Another Anglican acquaintance, a layman who coordinates his metropolitan Manchester's Alpha programme, similarly affirms that they have no shortage of takers for their parish's twice-yearly Alpha courses, each with two constituent groups of ten people. They even have a waiting list.

As part of a local church's strategy, Alpha is no longer the only tool in the mission toolbox, but it has proven to be one of the most effective, with support, literature and a track record in sharing the good news of Jesus.

Café church

In nearly every way, the café church phenomenon is the most unregulated or decentralised when compared with Messy Church or the highly organised Alpha programme. Café church began in the US. As the name clearly suggests, the format involves attendees sitting around tables and being served coffee, soft drinks and other light refreshments. Music is performed by guest singers and musicians (although they may be members of the host church), either live or on a big-screen recording, and the teaching is seemingly interactive, with guests bringing up current media stories with the pastor or leader, who responds with a biblical perspective.

My few experiences of café church in the US made me very uncomfortable, as each time I found the (different) pastor's grinning response, with a bludgeoning 'Am I right, or am I right?' (or similar put-down), far too magisterial, frustrating true interaction and conversation. Equally, uber-slick musical presentation meant that I felt I had been at the receiving end of an unwanted performance. Did I really believe the pastor was that good and biblically knowledgeable that his questioners had not been previously primed, even chosen?

I have friends in both Pennsylvania and Wisconsin, where their local church hosts a version of café church on one Sunday morning and a different Sunday evening each month; they independently discerned this programme timing. Both sets of friends are part of Mennonite churches, where the musicians and singers are good but regularly part of those congregations. In the one congregation, the pastor sits on a tall bar stool, acting as MC, inviting other café church guests to share in the responses or offer other biblical perspectives to the issue raised. In the other congregation, which lacks a full-time pastor, three elders with radio microphones gently prowl the central open space within the concentric circles of tables, reacting to one another as they offer responses to the questioner, before requesting supplementary questions from other guests. Is it because I am virtually a Mennonite, as an Anabaptist, that I believe these two models seem easier to translate to our UK context? Or is it because they are simpler, less slick in their styling and more truly conversational in discerning God's perspective?

Having said all this, my reaction to various UK expressions of café church has always been more positive than negative.

- Anglican acquaintances in a rural north Yorkshire (multi-congregation) united benefice only see their vicar for one Sunday morning service each month. So the gifted chair of the parochial church council leads the public conversation and two singers, a flautist and a pianist provide the music, in various configurations, for another Sunday's café church.
- In Wolverhampton, my ageing parents attend an ecumenical Thursday morning prayer breakfast, which is a café church in all but name and advertising. Recorded music, chosen for its topicality, is played, and each week's meditation and intercessions focus upon a major current news theme. The interactive discussion takes place around the several breakfast tables.
- As I already mentioned in Chapter 4, a Baptist village chapel in west Oxfordshire runs a monthly café church with cooked breakfasts, inviting villagers to bring their Sunday newspapers and discuss the ethical challenges of the headlining stories.
- Near to Cirencester another village chapel – united Congregational and Methodist – does a similar thing. This is not imitation but others recognising a God-given opportunity.
- Friends of mine in north London attend a fortnightly brunch café church, often with a jazz trio and occasionally a chanteuse, taking their Sunday papers with them, not knowing which local Christian minister will be MC and fielding that noontide discussion. Most of those friends have given up traditional denominational Christianity in favour of this café owner's more vibrant initiative. It turns out that all the jazzers were also once involved in traditionalist Christianity but have opted in favour of such a café church… where everyone buys their own brunch.

Clearly, I want to affirm all these café church initiatives as genuinely church. At the risk of repeating myself, the church is not like defining a cow as an animal with a leg at each corner that moos. It was one of the foundational leaders of the Churches of Christ who wrote, 'the church is *essentially, intentionally and constitutionally* one, whenever it gathers'.[28] This is a clear echo of Jesus' own injunction that 'wherever two or three gather in my name, there I am with them' (Matthew 18:20, NIV). The church is not called to conform to a particular four-legged framework, but obedience to the intentions of the living God whom we know in Jesus by the power of the Holy Spirit. Therefore, whether it is an Alpha meeting, a Messy Church gathering, a café church or even a Christian book group or deliberate eat-pray-tell shared meal, we have gathered under the reign of God, in the name of Jesus and we are as 'church', however imperfect, estranged or sinful the participants may be.

Christian book groups

I used to be part of a secular book group that met monthly, until I, along with another member (who was a Quaker), got a bit fed up with some of the salacious fiction or cheesy biographies that were voted for. We ended up leaving the group amicably, and I happened to recount this learning experience at a discipleship conference. Several of that conference's participants told me that either they or their congregation ran Christian book groups, in which participants choose what they want to read, rather than it be prescribed by the vicar, elder or some other church leader. At a later seminar at the same conference, when I was speaking about hospitality and eating together, I mentioned Christian book groups – and I started another learning journey. Perhaps because I had been stressing the importance of 'sharing food', all my subsequent correspondents about Christian book groups have been at pains to tell me how they share a meal together each time they gather. As my database of such contacts grows let me share a few examples:

- In Birmingham, it was my privilege to be at the meal when an Anabaptist-oriented group committed itself to meet monthly, share a meal, discuss a chapter of an agreed book of discipleship, then pray together. They agreed to do this initially for a year to build the relationships of people among the group before committing to inviting newcomers to join them on this journey.
- In Stroud, a Quaker couple run a monthly Christian book group with food, focusing on one book each school term, but ending each evening's gathering with silence around a lit candle.
- Near Brighton, a shared household with a variety of ecumenical backgrounds reaches out to isolated members of the gay community with its monthly supper and Christian book study evening.
- In Jesmond, Newcastle, a group of liberal Roman Catholics host a similar evening for as many of their contacts as can attend. Folks bring and share hot food in winter and they barbecue together in the summer, but the evening is also brought together by one regular participant introducing a particular, pre-agreed Christian book.
- One isolated Anglican parish in rural Herefordshire shares a vicar, receiving his Sunday ministry only once per month. On another Sunday, they run a Christian book group, with intercessions, after a shared breakfast as an 'alternative Sunday worship'. A few times each year, they invite the writer of a different book to join with them; I am one such writer to be blessed by their invitation.

The truth is that rightly no one is keeping score or records of this new Spirit-led, grass-roots initiative, but it is a good one. We should just note it, because I am increasingly aware that such Christian book groups include both the mature in faith and the newcomer in their gatherings. It is another eat, pray, tell with a twist.

How much is this the shape of things to come?

Eat, pray, tell, Messy Church, Alpha, café church and Christian book groups are all church in their own way. They may not have the fullness of expression that the all-singing, dancing, Eucharistic congregation does, but they are still vital activist missionary communities in which folk gather, get fed, are prayed for (sometimes over) and are learning to journey together within Jesus' words and ways. How is that *not* church?

One of the exciting things for me is that all these new expressions of church are rediscovering the vibrancy of the post-Pentecost early church and the pre-Christendom counterculturalism of shared dynamic faith. Both periods, and the time in between, were epitomised by the sharing of meals by women and men, of all races, poor and rich, as Jesus' egalitarian community took shape. Each of these 21st-century expressions of church are using meals to act as the glue to create community, not the false bonhomie of a quick coffee and stale biscuit after Sunday morning worship – however vibrant or arid the latter post-worship can become. In the use of shared meals to (re)build community, groups are subconsciously reshaping themselves in the mould of the countercultural early church. Previously, I quoted Alan Kreider's searches in early church primary sources, establishing this pattern of meal-sharing as factually accurate.[29]

Any of these new expressions of mission activity could enable a new community of believers, effectively a new church, to be forged upon the anvil of food, prayer and discussion shared. But that will only happen if we meet people where they *are* – and not where we believe they *should be*. Stuart Murray in his helpfully foundational book *Church Planting* says, 'New churches have been planted, at least in part, in order to allow Christians to rediscover the subversive memory of Jesus and to explore the implications of his teachings in their communal life.'[30] Do you recall that the former Archbishop of Canterbury saw this 'subversion' as a vital part of shared Christian life?

You may find that you disagree with my eat-pray-tell thesis. But many local congregations are ageing, not growing significantly and therefore slowly dying. Particularly in smaller congregations, their leadership teams need to undertake some urgent prayerful discernment. I know many congregations in retirement communities that simply do not have the personnel to run children's work, a choir or a lunch club. They need to find an initiative, just *one*, that can kick-start their mission and outreach. The various expressions of eat, pray, tell could provide that one vital opportunity. A generation ago, two highly experienced church consultants (and personal friends of mine) wrote, 'In the ecology of mission, it will not be enough for only one type of church to be mobilised for mission. It will require the efforts of many churches of all types to make the kind of missionary inroads that our continent requires.'[31] Their words are even more applicable today than when they were first published in 1993.

Please let go of your disagreement and recognise there is room for us all in God's ecology of mission. We need 'horses for courses' and different kinds of churches and mission expressions. Not all churches have the premises or personnel to run Alpha or Messy Church, but most can facilitate at least one or two couples to lead home-based eat-pray-tell initiatives as well as supportively pray for them and each of their gatherings. Eat, pray, tell will not work if it is a top-down demand, but only if it comes from the grass roots. Recall the discernment of missionary bishop Lesslie Newbigin that Jesus entrusted his story and his salvation to his new, egalitarian community. That community can only do what it can do through the power and prompting of the Holy Spirit. If that is Messy Church, café church or Alpha then so be it, and thank you Lord for enabling them to do it. Not all of us can be that idealised four-legged church that moos.

The world-renowned theologian Jürgen Moltmann has spent decades analysing and explaining the church and its mission. Ultimately, he recognises that although state or established or large institutional churches *may* survive, it is in the small, Spirit-led grass-roots initiatives where the *missio Dei* through the life of the church will be most effective. Moltmann envisages this as 'reform of the community from below. There is a wide diversity of attempts and approaches here, but we will pick out the "grassroots communities"… in recent years, "grass-roots communities" have grown up almost simultaneously in different countries and denominations…'[32]

It is not just me that believes that grass-roots expressions, like eat, pray, tell, are a vital part of *missio Dei*. That last phrase might sound scary, but having the same few folks around for supper is not meant to be scary, but life-enhancing, for everyone – including you!

Thanks to God's redeeming grace and the enlivening of the Spirit, the shape of God's people to come rests in the hands, hearts and vision of those who have come to know Jesus as brother, exemplar, saviour and Lord. We share an adventure in faith as we follow the words, works and ways of Jesus.

As you look back over this book, but particularly this final chapter, what is it that has struck you? Has it been the gift of creating community which the sharing of meals brings? Has it been the rich ecumenical diversity of the examples quoted? Or has it been the fact that many of these are initiatives from the grass roots, which almost anyone can be part of? Why not you?

We do not fulfil the great commission by sitting and watching others. We can easily move from being innocent bystanders to share in eat, pray, tell, knowing that it was Jesus' way of mission too.

Afterword

At the outset of this book, I pointed out that we all eat, and we all need to eat. The very fact that you are on this page means that you are someone who reads books and wants to know more about eat, pray, tell. But eat, pray, tell is ultimately not about reading theory, it is the practical sharing of food with others who may start out as strangers but become friends on the journey of following after Jesus. It nurtures relationships and creates community.

Jesus is our brother, exemplar, saviour and Lord. At several points in this book, we have reviewed some of both Jesus' and the New Testament church's practices of eat, pray, tell. Think afresh how Jesus prayerfully prepared for ministry: he nurtured relationships and created a new community. Remember how much Jesus must have become part of Peter's household and family to be allowed into Peter's mother-in-law's bedroom (Matthew 8:14). Think how much Lazarus and his sisters, Martha and Mary, and their Bethany home meant to Jesus; such deep friendships are only built up over much time and many shared meals (Luke 10:40; John 11). Why did the gathering at Emmaus only recognise Jesus when they sat at table and Jesus broke bread with them, if he had not done this so many times before (Luke 24:13-35)?

Eat, pray, tell is a transformative discipleship experience – in this, we share in Jesus' way of mission.

Let me close with a personal reflection, which some readers might already know. In 2007, I was hospitalised with a virally caused terminal heart condition, but thanks to much prayer (by many) and medical skill I survived, with a chronic life-limiting cardiomyopathy.

After more than a year's sick leave, I was forced to prematurely retire from a joyful, vibrant ministry, which wrecked all my retirement planning at huge personal cost. After the initial shock, I was angry with God that I had been robbed. It took the rich hospitality and many meal-time conversations of my family, my 'brothers in alms',[33] close friends (see page 5) and Anabaptist/Mennonite *companeros*[34] to make me realise that God was giving me a new life through eat, pray, tell.

Given an abundance of time, I successfully finished my Princeton (USA) doctorate about Christian meal-sharing. Janice came gently into my life, and together we explored different patterns of small group hospitality, gradually recognising it as eat, pray, tell. I began writing more fully – books and poetry as well as magazine articles. Released from particularly the weekend obligations of parochial ministry, I had been given time and many invitations to share the eat-pray-tell vision with others, at Saturday conferences and Sunday worship across Britain. Once again, I have an allotment; we make jams and chutneys, baking much of our own bread, thus eating a seasonal 'earth friendly' diet. Our lifestyle enriches the examples used in our teaching and travel as we move from Iona and other retreat houses, through Greenbelt and other festivals or conferences, through to the joy of learning with local congregations. As one of my 'brothers in alms' tells me, mine has become a 'life in three halves'.

Only now, can I look back and realise how God has blessed my life, renewed my ministry and inspired my writing in the simplicity of life which I share with Janice. Sometimes, I wish I had realised eat, pray, tell with others during my stipendiary ministry for more than that previous generation of service. But true discipleship is what God gives us today, like the manna in the wilderness (Exodus 16), and calls us to *now*, knowing contentment in that provision and obedience in God's call for this moment.

Eat, pray, tell has become my transformative discipleship experience in retirement, and what a great preparation for the heavenly banquet, too. Perhaps, however old you are, eat, pray, tell will become so for you as well, and in that for others, too.

Thank you, Lord.

Shalom.

Hallelujah and Amen.

Further reading

David Adam, *Borderlands* (SPCK, 1991).

Allan Armstrong, *Spiritualize your Life: What every Christian should know* (Imagier, 2017).

Robert and Julia Banks, *The Church Comes Home: Building community and mission through home churches*, revised edition (Hendrickson, 1998).

Andrew Francis, *Hospitality and Community after Christendom* (Paternoster, 2012).

Andrew Francis, *Shalom: The Jesus manifesto* (Paternoster, 2016).

Andrew Francis, *What in God's Name Are You Eating?* (Cascade, 2014).

Michael Green, *Evangelism through the Local Church* (Hodder and Stoughton, 1990).

Bill Hybels, *Too Busy Not to Pray* (IVP, 1994).

Alan Kreider, *The Patient Ferment of the Early Church* (Baker Academic, 2016).

Alan and Eleanor Kreider, *Worship and Mission after Christendom* (Paternoster, 2009).

Noel Moules, *Fingerprints of Fire, Footprints of Peace; A Spiritual Manifesto from a Jesus Perspective* (Circle Books, 2012).

Stuart Murray, *Changing Mission: Learning from the newer churches* (CTBI, 2006).

Lesslie Newbigin, *Truth to Tell: The gospel as public truth* (SPCK, 1991).

Edmund Newell (ed.), *Seven Words for the 21st Century* (Darton, Longman and Todd, 2002).

Phyllis Pellman Good and Louise Stoltzfus, *The Best of Mennonite Fellowship Meals* (Good Books, 1991).

Christine D. Pohl, *Making Room: Recovering hospitality as a Christian tradition* (Eerdmans, 1999).

Andrew Roberts, *Holy Habits* (Malcolm Down Publishing, 2016).

Notes

1   Tom Stuckey, *Into the Far Country* (Epworth Press, 2003).
2   Christine D. Pohl, *Making Room: Recovering hospitality as a Christian tradition* (Eerdmans, 1999), and *Living into Community: Cultivating practices that sustain us* (Eerdmans, 2012); Josh Hunt, *Christian Hospitality: An ancient practice that can refresh your life, revitalise your church and reach the world* (2012); Douglas Webster, *Table Grace: The role of hospitality in the Christian life* (Christian Focus Publications, 2011); Letty M. Russell, *Just Hospitality: God's welcome in a world of difference* (Westminster John Knox Press, 2009); Arthur M. Russell, *I Was a Stranger: A theology of hospitality* (Abingdon Press, 2006); Tim Chester, *A Meal with Jesus* (Crossway, 2011); Andrew Roberts, *Holy Habits* (Malcolm Down Publishing, 2016).
3   Andrew Francis, *Hospitality and Community after Christendom* (Paternoster, 2012).
4   Survey reported in the *Daily Telegraph*, 5 November 2009. For Messy Church, see www.messychurch.org.uk.
5   James R. Krabill and Stuart Murray, *Forming Christian Habits in Post-Christendom* (Herald Press, 2011).
6   John Dominic Crossan, *Jesus and the Violence of Scripture: How to read the Bible and still be a Christian* (SPCK, 2015).
7   Lesslie Newbigin, *Truth To Tell: The Gospel as public truth* (SPCK, 1991), p. 6.
8   Michael Green, *Evangelism through the Local Church* (Hodder and Stoughton, 1990), p. 289.
9   David Bosch, *Transforming Mission: Paradigm shifts in theology of mission* (Orbis, 1991), p. 472.
10 Bosch, *Transforming Mission*, pp. 517–519.
11 Rowan Williams in Ed Newell (ed.), *Seven Words for the 21st Century* (DLT, 2002), p. 3.

12 Rodney Clapp, *A Peculiar People: The church as culture in a post-Christian society* (IVP, 1996), p. 193.

13 David W. Shenk and Ervin R. Stutzman, *Creating Communities of the Kingdom* (Herald Press, 1988).

14 The *Ten… Churches* series was published by MARC Europe from the late 1970s into the 1980s. Each volume was multi-authored and under the guidance of different editors. All seem to be out of print, but many still appear in second-hand listings of online booksellers.

15 Walter Wink, *Unmasking the Powers* (Fortress Press, 1986), pp.82–83.

16 Robert Banks and Julia Banks, *The Church Comes Home: Building community and mission through home churches*, revised edition (Hendrickson, 1998), p. 154.

17 Stuart Murray, *Changing Mission: Learning from the newer churches* (CTBI, 2006), pp. 124–125.

18 Ched Myers, *Binding the Strong Man* (Orbis, 2003), p. 443; John Dominic Crossan, *Jesus: A revolutionary biography* (Harper San Francisco, 1994), p. 107; Pohl, *Making Room*, p. 154; John Howard Yoder, *Body Politics: Five practices of the Christian community before the watching world* (Discipleship Resources, 1992), p. 20.

19 Alan Kreider, *The Patient Ferment of the Early Church* (Baker Academic, 2016), p. 136.

20 See, for example, www.peacemeal.co.

21 Banks and Banks, *The Church Comes Home*.

22 Allan Armstrong, *Spiritualise Your Life: What every Christian should know* (Imagier, 2017), p. 132.

23 Bill Hybels, *Too Busy Not to Pray* (IVP, 1994).

24 Søren Kierkegaard, *The Quotable Kierkegaard*, ed. Gordon Merino (Princeton University Press, 2013), p. 97.

25 Oscar Cullmann, *The Johannine Circle* (SCM, 1976); Raymond Brown, *The Community of the Beloved Disciple* (Paulist Press, 1978).

26 George Lings (ed.), *Messy Church Theology* (BRF, 2013); Paul Moore, *Making Disciples in Messy Church: Growing faith in an all-age community* (BRF, 2013).

27 H.A. Hamilton, *The Family Church in Principle and Practice: A new setting for Christian education* (Epworth Press, 1941).

28 Alexander Campbell in his 'Declaration and address to the Churches

of Christ', quoted in David Thompson (ed.), *Stating the Gospel* (T&T Clark, 1989), pp. 118ff (italics in original).

29   Kreider, *The Patient Ferment*.

30   Stuart Murray, *Church Planting: Laying foundations* (Paternoster, 1998), p. 84.

31   Martin Robinson and Dan Yarnell, *Celebrating the Small Church* (Monarch, 1993), p. 11.

32   Jürgen Moltmann, *The Church in the Power of the Spirit* (Fortress Press, 1993), p. 328.

33   See the dedication in Andrew Francis, *Oikos: God's big word for a small planet* (Cascade, 2017).

34   See the dedication in Andrew Francis, *Shalom: The Jesus manifesto* (Paternoster, 2016).

Transforming
lives and communities

Christian growth and understanding of the Bible

Resourcing individuals, groups and leaders in churches for their own spiritual journey and for their ministry

Church outreach in the local community

Offering three programmes that churches are embracing to great effect as they seek to engage with their local communities and transform lives

Teaching Christianity in primary schools

Working with children and teachers to explore Christianity creatively and confidently

Children's and family ministry

Working with churches and families to explore Christianity creatively and bring the Bible alive

Visit **brf.org.uk** for more information on BRF's work
Review this book on Twitter using **#BRFconnect**

brf.org.uk

The Bible Reading Fellowship (BRF) is a Registered Charity (No. 233280)